COMPACT *Research*

Health Care

by Peggy J. Parks

Current Issues

ReferencePoint
Press™

San Diego, CA

© 2009 ReferencePoint Press, Inc.

For more information, contact:
ReferencePoint Press, Inc.
PO Box 27779
San Diego, CA 92198
www.ReferencePointPress.com

Picture credits:
AP Images: 12, 16
Steve Zmina: 31–34, 47–50, 64–67, 81–84

LIBRARY OF CONGRESS CATALOGING-IN-PUBLICATION DATA

Parks, Peggy J., 1951–
    Health care / by Peggy J. Parks.
        p. cm. — (Compact research)
    Includes bibliographical references and index.
    ISBN-13: 978-1-60152-068-5 (hardback)
    ISBN-10: 1-60152-068-9 (hardback)
    1. Medical care—United States. 2. Medical policy—United States. 3. Health care reform—
    United States. I. Title.
    RA395.A3P265 2008
    362.1—dc22
                                                                    2008040389

Contents

Foreword

Foreword

❝Where is the knowledge we have lost in information?❞

—T.S. Eliot, "The Rock."

As modern civilization continues to evolve, its ability to create, store, distribute, and access information expands exponentially. The explosion of information from all media continues to increase at a phenomenal rate. By 2020 some experts predict the worldwide information base will double every 73 days. While access to diverse sources of information and perspectives is paramount to any democratic society, information alone cannot help people gain knowledge and understanding. Information must be organized and presented clearly and succinctly in order to be understood. The challenge in the digital age becomes not the creation of information, but how best to sort, organize, enhance, and present information.

ReferencePoint Press developed the *Compact Research* series with this challenge of the information age in mind. More than any other subject area today, researching current issues can yield vast, diverse, and unqualified information that can be intimidating and overwhelming for even the most advanced and motivated researcher. The *Compact Research* series offers a compact, relevant, intelligent, and conveniently organized collection of information covering a variety of current topics ranging from illegal immigration and methamphetamine to diseases such as anorexia and meningitis.

The series focuses on three types of information: objective single-author narratives, opinion-based primary source quotations, and facts and statistics. The clearly written objective narratives provide context and reliable background information. Primary source quotes are carefully selected and cited, exposing the reader to differing points of view. And facts and statistics sections aid the reader in evaluating perspectives. Presenting these key types of information creates a richer, more balanced learning experience.

For better understanding and convenience, the series enhances information by organizing it into narrower topics and adding design features that make it easy for a reader to identify desired content. For example, in *Compact Research: Illegal Immigration*, a chapter covering the economic impact of illegal immigration has an objective narrative explaining the various ways the economy is impacted, a balanced section of numerous primary source quotes on the topic, followed by facts and full-color illustrations to encourage evaluation of contrasting perspectives.

The ancient Roman philosopher Lucius Annaeus Seneca wrote, "It is quality rather than quantity that matters." More than just a collection of content, the *Compact Research* series is simply committed to creating, finding, organizing, and presenting the most relevant and appropriate amount of information on a current topic in a user-friendly style that invites, intrigues, and fosters understanding.

Health Care at a Glance

Soaring Costs

In 2007 health care spending in the United States exceeded $2.2 trillion, up from $253 billion in 1980. This represented 16 percent of the gross domestic product (GDP).

Rising Insurance Premiums

The Kaiser Family Foundation reports that between 2000 and 2007 employer insurance premiums increased 87 percent, compared to cumulative inflation of 24 percent and estimated wage growth of 21 percent.

Those Who Suffer Most

Although the majority of Americans have some form of health insurance, either private or government funded, nearly 46 million are uninsured and tens of millions are underinsured.

How Health Care Dollars Are Spent

Of the total health care budget in 2007, $1.4 trillion was spent on hospital care and professional services, $231 billion on prescription drugs, $150 billion on investment and research, and $63 billion on government public health activities.

Taxpayer-Funded Insurance

An estimated 60 percent of the $2 trillion+ annual U.S. health care bill is paid by taxpayers at all income levels and is used to fund Medicare, Medicaid, and insurance for government employees.

Nationalized Health Care

The United States is the only industrialized country that does not pro-vide health insurance for all of its citizens. Many people believe that it is the government's responsibility to do so.

Quality of Care in America

Even though the United States spends more on health care than any other country, studies have shown that its health care quality lags behind other nations', and Americans' life expectancy ranks twenty-ninth in the world.

Fixing the Health Care System

Various plans have been proposed to reform America's health care system, including adopting a universal health care system such as in Germany or the Netherlands, expanding Medicare to cover everyone, providing tax cuts for health insurance costs, and universal health care vouchers.

Overview

&&The U.S. health care system is on a dangerous path, with a toxic combination of high costs, uneven quality, frequent errors, and limited access to care.&&

—Michael E. Porter and Elizabeth Olmsted Teisberg, *Redefining Health Care*.

&&Health care resembles an already over-sized teenager who keeps popping the financial seams on his clothing, is already the largest kid in the class, and gives every sign of continuing to grow until there isn't any space left in the room for anyone else.&&

—Henry J. Aaron, "Comments for Conference on Health Care Challenges Facing the Nation."

Many critics describe the health care system in the United States as a miserable failure, and they often point to people like Mark Windsor as an example of why. Windsor has accepted the fact that he is dying. Diagnosed with bone cancer more than 25 years ago, he has no health insurance because he is self-employed and cannot afford to purchase it. Before the cancer spread and advanced to the terminal stage, a few doctors donated their services to remove tumors, and Windsor believed that his disease was in remission. Then in the fall of 2006 the cancer returned, and he again needed surgery—but without insurance, that was not possible. He describes his frustrating attempts to find someone who was willing to help him: "All of a sudden I'm out here in this world with no hospital and no doctor. And everybody I faxed—I got on my computer and sent out e-mails and faxes to at least 20 neurosurgeons

8

in Atlanta and not a single one responded." At age 52, Windsor was too young to qualify for Medicare; and with an annual income of $30,000, he made too much money to qualify for Medicaid. He got married and his wife added him to her insurance policy, so he was able to undergo surgery in 2007 to remove a tumor on his neck. It was too late, however, as the tumor had been growing for 10 months and was very large, covering too much of his neck for surgeons to get all of it. Windsor has undergone post-surgery radiation therapy, but he knows it will merely prolong his life, not save it. After the treatment started, he learned that the insurance company had declined his claim for payment of medical bills, and now he is solely responsible for paying them. "I'm angry at the greed of the insurance companies," he says. "Everybody has the right to make profits. Every corporation has the right to be strong, make the right decisions. But I don't think that it is proper to deny people with chronic disease the opportunity to get well."[1]

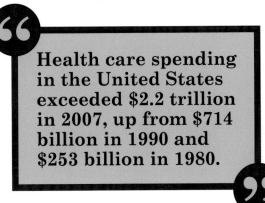

Health care spending in the United States exceeded $2.2 trillion in 2007, up from $714 billion in 1990 and $253 billion in 1980.

What Is the State of America's Health Care System?

Of all the issues facing legislators, economists, and business decision makers, health care is considered to be among the most critical. Health care spending in the United States exceeded $2.2 trillion in 2007, up from $714 billion in 1990 and $253 billion in 1980. Yet despite the continuously rising cost, the U.S. Census Bureau states that nearly 46 million Americans did not have health insurance in 2007, and tens of millions are underinsured. In August 2008 the Commonwealth Fund, a nonprofit group that monitors health care, released a survey about America's health care system. The report states that in 2007 nearly two-thirds of adults in the United States, or 116 million people, were either uninsured for a time during the year, were underinsured, reported a problem paying medical bills, and/or said they did not get needed health care because they could not afford it. A December 2007 report by the Centers for Disease Control and Prevention (CDC) reinforced the seriousness of America's health care situation, stating that nearly one out of five Americans needed but did not receive one or more services such as medical care, prescription medicines, mental health care, dental care, or eyeglasses because they could not pay for them. Jane Bryant Quinn, a journalist who specializes in financial issues, shares her thoughts: "America's health-care 'system' looks more like a lottery every year. The winners: the healthy and well insured, with good corporate coverage or Medicare. When they're ill, they get—as the cliché goes—'the best health care in the world.' The losers: those who rely on shrinking public insurance, such as Medicaid (nearly 45 million of us), or go uninsured (46 million and rising)."[2] For a variety of reasons, America's health care system is struggling and in need of radical change.

What Is the Cause of America's Health Care Situation?

The health care system in the United States has evolved over many years, and problems have developed along the way. It worked relatively well decades ago when medical care, dental care, hospitalization, and prescription drugs cost a fraction of what they do today, and nearly all Americans had health insurance furnished by their employers. Through the years, however, the cost of insurance has risen at rates that far surpass the rate of inflation and employee wages. As a result, many employers are reducing their health insurance benefits by passing along larger amounts to employees or even eliminating insurance altogether because they simply cannot afford to pay for it.

Another contributor to America's soaring health care price tag is the burgeoning population of elderly people, which has caused enormous growth in Medicare's enrollment. Even though the agency's administrative costs are much lower than those of private health insurers, Medicare spending has continued to rise over the years. In 1995 its annual cost was $218 billion, and by 2007 the cost had nearly doubled to $427 billion. As medical care continues to improve people's health and well-being, they will live longer than ever before, and this will further stretch Medicare's resources. Financial experts say that if this spending is not contained, Medicare's cost will be more than $500 billion by 2011.

Many people point to the growth of malpractice suits as a root cause of the health care problem in America. The number of lawsuits has climbed over the years, and as a result, the insurance premiums that medical professionals and hospitals must pay have also climbed. One example is New York–Presbyterian Hospital, which reports that between 2002 and 2006, its malpractice insurance costs doubled. The hospital currently spends $150 million a year—or between 3 and 4 percent of its total budget—on liability insurance. Similar situations are reported nationwide. According to Darrell E. White, a physician from Westlake, Ohio, "Doctors are highly incentivized to order extra care because of the risk of malpractice litigation. It has been estimated that 5% to 25% of our health care expenses are due to the practice of defensive medicine, ordering tests and procedures solely to avoid lawsuits."[3]

Who Suffers Most Under America's Health Care System?

One of the biggest flaws of the health care system in the United States is that so many people either have poor access to health care or no access at all. An estimated 80 percent of American workers have health insurance that is paid for, completely or in part, by their employers. Medicare covers those who are over the age of 65, as well as people under age 65 who have certain disabilities or end-stage kidney disease that requires either dialysis or a kidney transplant. Medicaid covers low-income children and adults, including an estimated 1.4 millon elderly people who receive long-term care in nursing homes. Many children whose parents' income is low but still too high to be eligible for Medicaid, are covered under the State Children's Health Insurance Program (SCHIP). The

> " Another contributor to America's soaring health care price tag is the burgeoning population of elderly people, which has caused enormous growth in Medicare's enrollment. "

Veterans Health Administration provides coverage to military veterans. Together, all those who either have private health insurance or qualify for some sort of federal health care assistance represent a sizable major-

On June 19, 2008, the California Nurses Association and other groups took part in a nationwide protest of America's health insurance plans. Because so many Americans cannot afford health insurance and do not have access to quality health care, reforming the health care system is a subject of major discussion.

ity of the population—approximately 254 million people, according to an August 2008 report by the U.S. Census Bureau. But millions are still falling through the cracks and do not have access to quality health care. They are the working poor, people who are not old enough and/or who make too much money to qualify for federal assistance, but who cannot afford to pay for health insurance. Consequently, they are often forced to choose between basic living expenses and paying for their health care out of pocket. Because their budgets are already stretched thin, they often forego medical and dental care for themselves and their families.

How Are America's Health Care Dollars Spent?

Health care spending in the United States encompasses a wide array of health-related goods and services. According to a report by the Centers for Medicare and Medicaid Services (CMS), the biggest share of the 2008 health expenditure budget—nearly $1.4 trillion—was spent on hospital care and professional (including physician, clinical, dental, and other) services. Another $247 billion was spent on prescription drugs, $160 billion was spent on investment and research, and $67.1 billion went for government public health activities.

Not called out in the CMS report is the exact amount of money that is spent on administrative costs. According to a 2004 study by researchers at Harvard Medical School, the United States spends nearly $400 billion per year on what the group calls "health care bureaucracy," including the administrative costs of health insurers, hospitals, nursing homes, home care agencies, physicians, and other practitioners. The authors claim that such bureaucracy accounts for at least 31 percent of total U.S. health care spending. Many health care experts say that a big reason why administrative costs are so high is the vast amount of time that medical professionals must spend on administrative duties, as Harvard Medical School professor David Himmelstein explains: "U.S. doctors face a . . . billing nightmare. They deal with hundreds of [insurance] plans, each with different rules and regulations, each allowing physicians to prescribe a different group of medications, each dictating that doctors refer patients to different specialists. The U.S. system is a paperwork nightmare for doctors and patients, and wastes hundreds of billions of dollars."[4]

Health Insurance, Courtesy of Taxpayers

Americans may not be aware of it, but they heavily subsidize the health care system—and this is true even for those who have no insurance or are not able to afford health care for themselves and their families. During 2008, $490 billion, which was collected from American taxpayers, was spent on funding Medicare and Medicaid. Yet federal health programs are only a part of the total financial picture. According to health consultant Joel A. Harrison, more than 60 percent of the $2 trillion+ annual U.S. health care bill is paid by taxpayers of all income levels in the United States. He explains:

> Almost no one recognizes that even people without health insurance pay substantial sums into the system today. . . . Tax dollars pay for Medicare and Medicaid, for the

Veterans Administration and the Indian Health Service. Tax dollars pay for health coverage for federal, state and municipal government employees and their families, as well as for many employees of private companies working on government contracts.[5]

Harrison adds that a person who earns an annual salary of $25,000 and has no health insurance of his or her own still pays more than $2,400 per year for the health care system—one that does not serve them. That is, Harrison states, "enough for a healthy young adult to purchase a year's worth of insurance."[6]

Should America's Health Care Be Nationalized?

Because so many Americans cannot afford health insurance and do not have access to quality health care, reforming the health care system is a subject of major discussion—but *how* that should be done is highly controversial. The United States is the only industrialized country in the world that does not provide some form of health care for all its citizens. Many are convinced that America should follow the lead of Great Britain and Canada and implement a nationalized program so that everyone would be covered. Those who favor a government-controlled health care system say that if major adjustments were made in the way health care dollars are currently spent, universal health care would easily be affordable. Quinn shares her perspective: "I do agree that we can't afford to cover everyone under the crazy health-care system we have now. We can't even afford all the people we're covering already, which is why we keep booting them out. But we have an excellent template for universal care right under our noses: good old American Medicare. When you think of reform, think 'Medicare for all.'"[7]

> **[The uninsured] are often forced to choose between basic living expenses and paying for their health care out of pocket.**

Those who are against nationalized health care argue that it is a form of socialism, meaning that the government is in control rather than a free market system in which health care is provided by the private sector. These opponents believe that any form of a nationalized system inevitably results in poor to mediocre quality, long waiting times, and rationing, and they refer to countries such as Great Britain to prove their point. Barrie Redfern, a man who formerly lived in England, shares his frustrating experience with the British National Health Service (NHS):

> After a motorcycle accident in Yorkshire I returned home with a wrist suffering multiple fractures. Sorry no x-ray facilities in my town after 6 P.M. Wait until next morning. Doctor admits it's too complicated and I need to check into another hospital a rail and bus ride away. Second hospital can't fix it as an out-patient. Finally admitted to a ward by 4 P.M. By midnight still no sign of action and threatened to leave. One A.M. and I am wheeled into the operating theatre. Left for home—by train lunchtime— nearly 24 hours after my accident. When I wrote to complain about it, far from apologising, the hospital had the audacity to say it was busy and I had to wait my turn. Well, if the NHS thinks this is normal then thank goodness I no longer live in Britain."[8]

Health Care Quality

For many years the United States was hailed as having the most excellent health care in the world, but recent studies have shown that this perception is flawed. Despite the astronomical amount of money that is spent on health care every year, Ezekiel J. Emanuel, a physician with the National Institutes of Health, says that the status of Americans' health "looks sickly when measured against the tallies of other industrialized countries," and he refers to the health care system as a "dysfunctional mess."[9] His reference to Americans being "sickly" was reinforced in a May 2007 report by the Commonwealth Fund. The authors of the study compared America's health care system with those of five other industrialized countries: Australia, Canada, Germany, New Zealand, and the United Kingdom. According to the report's authors, the United States ranked last, as it did in reports published in 2006 and 2004.

Marie Dreyer holds some of the medications she needs to treat a variety of illnesses. Dreyer, 57, has been rejected by health insurers because she suffers from fibromyalgia and high blood pressure.

Can People Be Denied Health Care If They Cannot Pay?

Many people argue that no one in America can be refused hospital care, and that is technically true. Since 1986, with the passage of the Emergency Medical Treatment and Active Labor Act (EMTALA), federal law has mandated that a hospital capable of providing care cannot turn away anyone who arrives at an emergency department, regardless of his or her ability to pay. Yet numerous studies have shown that people who lack health insurance, especially those in poor urban areas, often suffer for hours and hours as they wait for medical treatment—and some have died while waiting. This was the case with Esmin Green, who was taken by paramedics to the psychiatric emergency room of Kings County Hospital in New York City on June 18, 2007. Green was suffering from agitation and psychosis, and after refusing a medical review she was involuntarily admitted. She waited in the emergency room for nearly 24 hours before she collapsed in her chair and fell onto the floor. Footage from video cameras showed that no medical staff moved in to help her, even though a few passed by and saw her lying on the floor with her legs thrashing. She lay in that position for an hour before a nurse finally came to check her pulse and found that she had died.

> Americans may not be aware of it, but they heavily subsidize the health care system—and this is true even for those who have no insurance or are not able to afford health care for themselves and their families.

Another consideration is that even though poor people cannot legally be denied emergency care, they are still billed for the services provided to them and are often hounded by collection agencies when they do not pay. This can lead to financial ruin and a credit rating that is virtually destroyed. According to Harrison, 50 percent of consumer bankruptcies in the United States are the result of unpaid medical bills—and an estimated three-quarters of those people had at least some health insurance before they got sick.

How Can America Improve Its Health Care System?

Some argue that the health care system, as it exists now, is so broken that it cannot be fixed; instead, they say, it must be completely redesigned and rebuilt from the ground up. Others insist that health care could be fixed if the right program was in place. The Physicians for a National Health Program organization advocates a single-payer national health insurance that organizes health financing; in other words, that the federal government should pay health care providers directly but leave delivery of care largely a private matter. A growing number of people believe that the answer lies with Medicare; since the system is already in place and is largely successful, with low administrative costs, they believe it could be expanded to cover all Americans rather than just the elderly and the disabled. Emanuel supports the implementation of universal health care vouchers, which the federal government would issue to all Americans to purchase the health insurance of their choice. Still others believe that insurance companies are at the core of America's health care crisis and that whatever reform plan is adopted should eliminate the need for health insurance and eliminate insurers from the picture altogether. As would be expected, insurance companies adamantly reject this idea. Quinn writes: "Health insurers hate [the single-payer] model, which would end their gravy train."[10]

Health Care in the Future

With health care receiving so much attention and being such a hot topic of discussion, some sort of reform is inevitable in the future. But will it really solve the problem? And will it happen soon enough? As Democratic and Republican legislators engage in contentious and seemingly never-ending debates about the best way to fix America's health care system, tens of millions of people are still without medical and dental care for themselves and their families because they cannot afford it. And the future looks far worse. The Commonwealth Fund projects that the number of uninsured Americans is expected to rise to 56 million by 2013. Unless drastic measures are taken quickly, the future of America's health care system—and the people who depend on it—looks extremely bleak.

What Is the State of America's Health Care System?

> **America has the best health care system in the world, pure and simple. . . . We got the best medicines, we got the best doctors, and we have the best hospitals.**
>
> —George W. Bush, "President Discusses Health Care Initiatives."

> **What do we get for all that money? Politicians are constantly telling us we have the best health care in the world, but that's simply not the case.**
>
> —Shannon Brownlee, *AARP Magazine*.

The state of America's health care system has become one of the most widely discussed topics of the 21st century. Former and current legislators are giving speeches about health care, economists and journalists are writing about it, college professors are lecturing about it in their classrooms, and authors are publishing books about it. Innumerable viewpoints exist about what the problems are and what should be done to fix them, and highly controversial opinions are often publicly debated. Few would disagree, however, that the system is failing and needs a radical overhaul. "The combination of high costs, unsatisfactory quality, and limited access to health care has created anxiety and frustration for all participants," write Michael E. Porter and Elizabeth Olmsted Teisberg in their book *Redefining Health Care*.

No one is happy with the current system—not patients, who worry about the cost of insurance and the quality of care; not employers, who face escalating premiums and unhappy employees; not physicians and other providers, whose incomes have been squeezed, professional judgments overridden, and workdays overwhelmed with bureaucracy and paperwork; not health plans, which are routinely vilified; not suppliers of drugs and medical devices, which have introduced many life-saving or life-enhancing therapies but get blamed for driving up costs; and not governments, whose budgets are spinning out of control. Decades of "reform" have failed to improve the situation; if anything, matters have gotten worse.[11]

An Astronomical Sum

The amount of money that the United States spends on health care is so staggering that its magnitude is difficult to comprehend. In a February 8, 2008, broadcast on National Public Radio, author David M. Schwartz discussed the concept of $1 trillion and used an analogy to help explain what a massive amount that is. He stated that if one were to stack enough $100 bills to total $1 trillion, the pile of money would be 789 miles (1,270km) high. "Yeah," said Schwartz, "we're talking about real money."[12] Using the same analogy with a health care budget that exceeds $2.3 trillion, the stack of $100 bills would tower 1,815 miles (2,921km) high. Even more astounding is how the cost of health care has spiked over the years. According to an August 2007 report by the Kaiser Family Foundation, annual health care spending in 1970 was about $75 billion—which means that in fewer than 40 years the money spent on health care has increased *3,000 percent.*

> **The amount of money that the United States spends on health care is so staggering that its magnitude is difficult to comprehend.**

When people refer to the $2.3 trillion that the United States spends annually on health care, it may sound as though all the money is being spent by the government, but that is not the case. The total health care budget comprises expenditures from all sources, including not only the government but also insurance companies, private citizens, and businesses. According to statistics from the Centers for Medicare and Medicaid Services, in 2006, $851 billion of total health care spending came from private health insurance, while $828 billion was spent by Medicare and Medicaid. The additional breakdown includes $299 billion from out-of-pocket medical expenses, $230 billion from other public sources (including SCHIP, Workers Compensation, and the Veterans Administration), and $92 billion from other private sources such as charitable organizations and auto insurance payments for medical claims.

Are Costs Spiraling Out of Control?

Perspectives on why America's health care system is struggling so badly often differ based on personal opinion. Most experts agree that rather than one single cause, a combination of factors is involved. "It is hard to boil it down to one bogeyman,"[13] says internist Mark Smith, who is president of the California research group HealthCare Foundation. It is known, though, that health care costs are soaring at a rate that rapidly outpaces the rate of inflation.

One reason that costs are so high in the United States is the lack of centralized cost control. Unlike many countries in which medical costs are regulated by the government, America has no such cost control mechanism in place. When journalist David Asman and his wife were on vacation in England, she suffered a stroke and needed tests, hospitalization, and therapy sessions. Because he was not a British citizen, Asman was responsible for paying the bills, but when he received them he was shocked at how low they were. He explains:

> I thought there was a mistake. The bill included all doctors' costs, two MRI scans, more than a dozen physical therapy sessions, numerous blood and pathology tests, and of course room and board in the hospital for a month. And perhaps most important, it included the loving care of the finest nurses we'd encountered anywhere. The total cost: $25,752. That ain't chump change. But to put this in context, the cost of just 10 physical therapy sessions at New York's Cornell University Hospital came to $27,000.

. . . There is something seriously out of whack about 10 therapy sessions that cost more than a month's worth of hospital bills in England.[14]

One contributor to America's rising health care costs is the development of new medical procedures and technologies. Some economists say that as much as 50 percent of America's medical cost growth is due to new medical technologies, such as improved CT (computed tomography) and PET (positron emission tomography) scans. Both are sophisticated imaging tools that physicians use to pinpoint various types of diseases in the body, including cancer, heart disease, and brain disorders—and both are expensive. Each of the machines costs from $2 million to $4 million to install, and the cost for procedures ranges from $2,500 to $6,000. This amount varies widely from state to state, however, as well as from hospital to hospital. One woman wrote in an online breast cancer forum that the total bill for her PET/CT scans at Cedars-Sinai Medical Center in Los Angeles was nearly $18,000. According to the consulting firm Frost & Sullivan, more than 5 million PET scans alone will be performed annually by the year 2009.

> **The Kaiser Family Foundation states that between 2000 and 2007 employer insurance premiums spiked 87 percent, compared to cumulative inflation of 24 percent and estimated wage growth of 21 percent during the same period.**

Although drugs represent a small percentage of overall health care spending, that may not be the case for very long because their prices are continuing to rise. According to Henry J. Aaron of the Brookings Institution, drugs have been claiming an ever-increasing share of the health care budget since 1982, and this also contributes to health care's soaring costs. Matthew Perrone of the Associated Press states that the highest cost hikes are for specialized drugs that are used to treat rare ailments. For example, Ovation Pharmaceuticals raised the price of a drug known as Cosmegen, prescribed for children with kidney cancer, more than 3,400 percent in 2006. The price of Abbott Laboratories' HIV drug Norvir has risen by 400 percent. Health correspondent Susan Dentzer states that the drug Urbatux, which is used to treat patients with colon cancer, costs $100,000 a year.

The Role of Health Insurers

When discussing America's health care problems, many pin the blame on insurance companies. An estimated 1,500 different health insurers exist in America today, each of whom offers multiple plans, has its own enrollment requirements, its own marketing program, and its own administrative costs—and the latter accounts for a huge chunk of the cost of health insurance. According to a January 2006 report by Merrill Matthews of the Council for Affordable Health Insurance, administrative costs for insurers of large groups average 12.5 percent, while for individual policies the cost is 30 percent. Experts do not always agree about the administrative costs for Medicare; Quinn states that its overhead is less than 2 percent, while Matthews says that it is somewhere between 5.2 and 8 percent. This is still significantly lower than private health insurance.

Atlanta internist Orville Campbell describes insurance companies as having "a stranglehold on doctors and other healthcare providers and the delivery of healthcare." Campbell adds that "a significant number of these health insurance companies get richer and richer; their buildings get taller and taller and they become more powerful political lobbyists."[15] Critics say that insurers continue to grow richer and more profitable at the expense of consumers, a growing number of whom cannot afford the premiums. The Kaiser Family Foundation states that between 2000 and 2007 employer insurance premiums spiked 87 percent, compared to cumulative inflation of 24 percent and estimated wage growth of 21 percent during the same period. Currently, General Motors (GM) spends more for employee and retiree health insurance than it does for steel, and insurance benefits add an estimated $1,600 to the price of every vehicle that GM builds. Businesses all over the United States face the same problem. Because the cost of health insurance has been so prohibitive, many employers, especially those who own small- to medium-size businesses, have stopped offering health insurance altogether. Others have reduced benefits for employees while raising deductibles and co-pays.

Even as insurance premiums have continued to rise, health insurers have stepped up their efforts to increase denial of coverage claims, leaving thousands of formerly insured people without insurance. This was the case with Nataline Sarkisyan, a 17-year-old girl from Glendale, California, whose insurer (Cigna HealthCare) rejected a claim for a lifesaving operation. Nataline suffered from leukemia and had developed serious complications following a bone marrow transplant. Her liver failed, and doctors said that the only way she would survive was to undergo an emergency liver transplant. Even though the girl was fully insured and a matching donor had been found, Cigna stated on December 11, 2007, that it would not cover the operation because its benefit plan did not cover "experimental, investigational and unproven services."[16] Just the down payment alone for the surgery was $75,000, and the Sarkisyan family could not afford to pay it. Physicians and other health care professionals began bombarding Cigna offices throughout the country with letters and telephone calls, demanding that the decision be reversed. Their request was granted on December 19, but it was too late. Nataline died just a few hours later, and her family was convinced that the insurance company was solely to blame for her death.

> " Although millions of people in America are uninsured, those who have comprehensive health insurance policies are often oblivious to actual health care costs. "

Unnecessary Health Care

Although millions of people in America are uninsured, those who have comprehensive health insurance policies are often oblivious to actual health care costs. For them, the price of a doctor's visit, prescription drugs, and hospitalization is limited to their co-pay and deductibles. Economists say that if people were not so insulated from health care costs, they would be forced to compare medical services and shop accordingly. Journalists John Stossel and Andrew Sullivan explain: "When we pay for health care with someone else's money, it creates nasty incentives. . . . When patients pay for almost everything from physicals to acupuncture using third-party money, they have no reason to care about cost. Because the buyers don't care about cost, neither do the health-care providers."[17]

This sort of reasoning explains a theory known as moral hazard, which holds that when people are unconcerned about having to pay for health care, they naturally consume more than they normally would. Medical journalist Shannon Brownlee describes the theory: "Moral hazard says we go to the doctor when we don't really need to; we insist on getting a CT scan for a twisted ankle when ice and an Ace bandage will do. Experts will tell you that as many as one in four doctor's-office visits are 'social calls,' and nearly half of emergency room visits are for care that could have been handled in a nonemergency setting." Brownlee goes on to say that the most significant reason Americans are "drowning in health care debt" is that too many are receiving unnecessary care. "Of our total $2.3 trillion health care bill [in 2007]," she writes, "a whopping $500 billion to $700 billion was spent on treatments, tests, and hospitalizations that did nothing to improve our health."[18]

Tough Choices

With America's health care system being such a highly publicized issue, it is getting more attention than ever before, which is a positive development. Although economists, legislators, employers, and other decision makers often disagree about the severity of the problem, they do agree that reform is essential—because if reform does not happen, more and more adults and children in the United States will lose access to the health care that they need. But no one doubts that many questions remain. How badly damaged is the system? Is it as bad as many experts say it is? Why do the current problems exist? Can costs be brought under control? Are insurance companies part of the problem or part of the solution? Hopefully, for the sake of all Americans, these questions will be answered in the not-too-distant future.

What Is the State of America's Health Care System?

66 Individual freedom and personal choice, rooted in American values, provide principled health care, moral health care, and the best health care. That is why it is the best in the world. 99

—Richard E. Ralston, "American Health Care: The Best in the World," Americans for Free Choice in Medicine, September 19, 2006. www.afcm.org.

Ralston is executive director of Americans for Free Choice in Medicine.

66 Once upon a time, it was taken as an article of faith among most Americans that the U.S. health care system was simply the best in the world. Yet growing evidence indicates the system falls short given the high level of resources committed to health care. 99

—Commonwealth Fund, "Why Not the Best? Results from a National Scorecard on U.S. Health System Performance," September 20, 2006. www.commonwealthfund.org.

Commonwealth Fund is a private foundation that monitors health care in the United States.

Bracketed quotes indicate conflicting positions.

* Editor's Note: While the definition of a primary source can be narrowly or broadly defined, for the purposes of Compact Research, a primary source consists of: 1) results of original research presented by an organization or researcher; 2) eyewitness accounts of events, personal experience, or work experience; 3) first-person editorials offering pundits' opinions; 4) government officials presenting political plans and/or policies; 5) representatives of organizations presenting testimony or policy.

> **Experts agree that our health care system is riddled with inefficiencies, excessive administrative expenses, inflated prices, poor management, and inappropriate care, waste and fraud.**

—National Coalition on Health Care, "Health Insurance Costs," 2008. www.nchc.org.

The National Coalition on Health Care, which is composed of more than 70 organizations, is an alliance that seeks to improve America's health care system and ensure better, more affordable health care for everyone.

> **Although the high cost of health care is a frequently heard complaint, it is important to note that a substantial portion of the cost increases that we have seen in recent decades reflects improvements in both the quality and quantity of care delivered.**

—Ben S. Bernanke, "Challenges for Health-Care Reform," speech at the Senate Finance Committee Health Reform Summit, Washington, D.C., June 16, 2008. www.federalreserve.gov.

Bernanke is chairman of the U.S. Federal Reserve Bank.

> **The U.S. health care system is notorious for its high costs, which Americans traditionally assumed was the price of excellence. . . . There is compelling evidence that much care falls well short of excellence, that both too little and too much care is provided, and that alarming rates of medical error persist.**

—Michael E. Porter and Elizabeth Olmsted Teisberg, *Redefining Health Care*. Boston: Harvard Business School Press, 2006, p. 1.

Porter is the Bishop William Lawrence University Professor at Harvard Business School, and Teisberg is a professor at the University of Virginia's Darden Graduate School of Business.

> **The American health system: Expensive and worth every penny.**

—Don Surber, "More Proof U.S. Health Care Is the Best," *Daily Mail* blog, September 30, 2007. http://blogs.dailymail.com.

Surber is a political commentator and columnist for the *Charleston Daily Mail*.

66 The public knows the American health-care system is breaking up, no matter how much its backers cheer. For starters, there's the 46 million uninsured (projected to rise to 56 million in five years).99

—Jane Bryant Quinn, "Yes, We Can All Be Insured," *Newsweek*, August 15, 2007. www.newsweek.com.

Quinn is a journalist and contributing editor to *Newsweek* who specializes in financial issues and money management.

66 Yet another myth is that although the United States spends more on health care, we don't get more.99

—John Goodman, "Five Myths of Socialized Medicine," *Cato's Letter*, Winter 2005. www.cato.org.

Goodman is the founder and president of the National Center for Policy Analysis in Dallas, Texas.

66 We spend more and more money [on health care] with nothing to show for it. What's wrong with our system?99

—Lewis Miller, "Is America's Health Care System Failing?" *Health Commentary*, July 21, 2008. healthcommentary.org.

Miller is corporate editorial director of Dowden Health Media and cofounder and principal of the consulting firm WentzMiller & Associates.

66 The fundamental problem in the U.S. health care system is that the structure of health care delivery is broken. . . . And the structure of health care delivery is broken because competition is broken.99

—Michael E. Porter and Elizabeth Olmsted Teisberg, *Redefining Health Care*. Boston: Harvard Business School Press, 2006, p. 3.

Porter is the Bishop William Lawrence University Professor at Harvard Business School, and Teisberg is a professor at the University of Virginia's Darden Graduate School of Business.

66 The fundamental cause of the high cost of health care in the U.S. is the deranged structure of the health care system. 99

—David Himmelstein, interviewed by Nancy Welch, "The Health Care Crisis in America," *Counter Punch*, October 30–31, 2004. www.counterpunch.org.

Himmelstein teaches at Harvard Medical School and is a cofounder of Physicians for a National Health Program.

66 America has the best health care in the world and we must work to keep it so, but we must also work to provide incentives to control costs and thereby make that care more accessible. 99

—John McCain, "Address to Detroit Economic Club," October 9, 2007. www.johnmccain.com.

McCain is a U.S. senator from Arizona and also the 2008 Republican nominee for president.

66 Lessons from the experiences of other nations are certainly available, but most Americans are ignorant of them and still believe claims that 'our system is the best.' 99

—Jon Basil Utley, "How Hospital Costs Ran Amok," *Reason*, August 4, 2008. www.reason.com.

Utley is associate publisher of *The American Conservative* and a former insurance executive with AIG.

Facts and Illustrations

What Is the State of America's Health Care System?

- In 2007 health care spending in the United States exceeded **$2.2 trillion**, up from $75 billion in 1970.

- In 1960 health care spending represented **5.2 percent** of the GDP; by 2007 it had risen to **16 percent**.

- The Congressional Budget Office reports that in the past 30 years, health care spending in the United States rose **2 percent** faster annually than the rest of the economy.

- Health care is the **largest sector of the American economy**; according to the Centers for Medicare and Medicaid Services, the amount spent on health care is higher than what is spent on housing, food, and national defense.

- The amount that the United States spends on health care each year is equivalent to the entire **economy of China**.

- The Kaiser Family Foundation states that employer health insurance premiums spiked **87 percent** between 2000 and 2007.

- The vast majority of America's health spending is for care provided by **hospitals and physicians**.

Health Care Funding and Expenditures

The estimated $2.2 trillion that the United States spends on health care comes from various public and private sources. In terms of how the money is spent, the vast majority goes for hospital care and professional services. These charts show the breakdown.

Where the Money Comes From

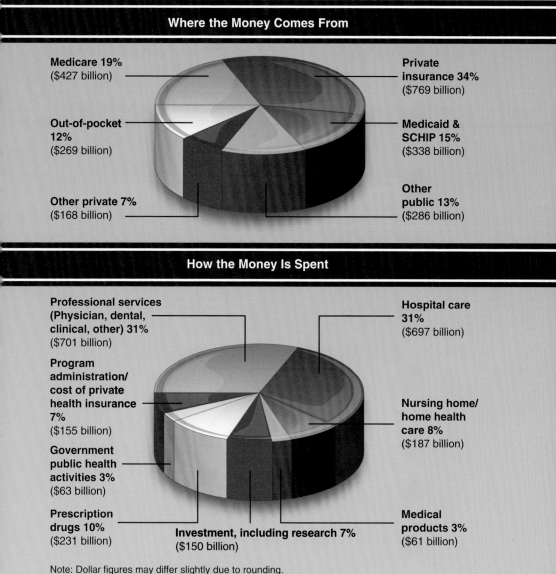

Medicare 19%
($427 billion)

Private insurance 34%
($769 billion)

Out-of-pocket 12%
($269 billion)

Medicaid & SCHIP 15%
($338 billion)

Other private 7%
($168 billion)

Other public 13%
($286 billion)

How the Money Is Spent

Professional services (Physician, dental, clinical, other) 31%
($701 billion)

Hospital care 31%
($697 billion)

Program administration/ cost of private health insurance 7%
($155 billion)

Nursing home/ home health care 8%
($187 billion)

Government public health activities 3%
($63 billion)

Prescription drugs 10%
($231 billion)

Investment, including research 7%
($150 billion)

Medical products 3%
($61 billion)

Note: Dollar figures may differ slightly due to rounding.

Source: Centers for Medicare & Medicaid Services, "National Health Expenditure Projections, 2007–2017," February 27, 2008. www.cms.hhs.gov.

- According to the American College of Physicians, about **10 percent** of the American population incurs from **60 to 70 percent** of all health care costs.

- In 1995 Medicare's annual cost was $218 billion; by 2006 the cost had risen to **$374 billion**.

Health Care's Share of the U.S. Economy

Of all the components of America's economy, health care is the largest sector. As a percentage of gross domestic product (GDP), more money is spent on health care than on housing, food, and national defense.

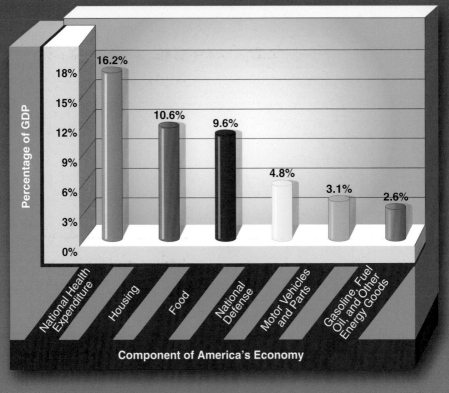

Source: Blue Cross and Blue Shield Association, "Healthcare Financing Trends," 2008 Medical Cost Reference Guide. www.bcbs.com.

American Health Care Quality Drops

Even as health care costs have continued to spike in the United States, a 2008 scorecard by the Commonwealth Fund (a private foundation that aims to promote a high-performing health care system that offers better access, higher quality, and greater efficiency, particularly for society's most vulnerable) shows that the country is falling short of achieving important benchmarks for quality and other measures of performance.

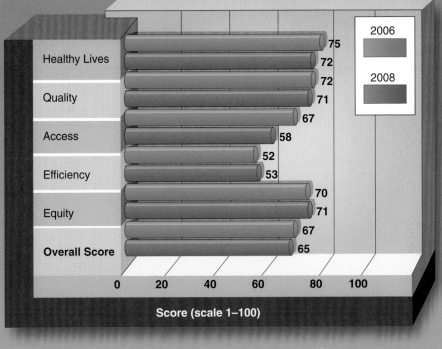

Source: The Commonwealth Fund, "Why Not the Best?" July 2008. www.commonwealthfund.org.

- A study released in September 2008 by Families USA shows that family health insurance premiums have steadily risen throughout the United States, with some states having enormous spikes; in New Mexico, for instance, workers' premiums rose **92.3 percent** between 2000 and 2007; in Pennsylvania the increase was more than **86 percent**, and Indiana's premiums rose **83.4 percent**.

The Steady Growth of Health Care Spending

The amount that the United States spends on health care is staggering—more than $2.2 trillion in 2007, up from $75 billion in 1970. This graph shows how per-capita spending has risen over the years, and its increasing share of gross domestic product (GDP).

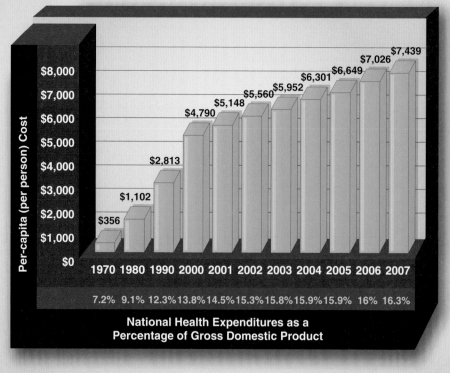

National Health Expenditures as a Percentage of Gross Domestic Product

Sources: Centers for Medicare & Medicaid Services, "National Health Expenditure Projections, 2007–2017," February 27, 2008. www.cms.hhs.gov; Kaiser Family Foundation, "Health Care Costs: A Primer," August 2007. www.kff.org.

- According to the American College of Physicians, the Institute of Medicine has documented high levels of **medical errors** and **inappropriate and unnecessary care**, which it says is indicative of systemwide problems with delivering consistently high-quality care.

- An August 2007 report by the Kaiser Family Foundation states that prescription drug costs account for **10 percent** of total health care spending but **14 percent** of the total growth in health care spending.

Who Suffers Most Under America's Health Care System?

66 Today there are 46 million uninsured Americans. These people neither receive insurance through an employer nor qualify for one of the government's two major public health insurance programs. Yet many of the uninsured are employed. . . . These uninsured Americans rely on a combination of charity, bad debt, and out-of pocket healthcare. 99

—Nicholas Pulos, "An Ethnographic Look at Healthcare Choices of the Working Poor."

66 For the working poor, everything hinges on being able to go to work and earn a paycheck. Getting sick just gets in the way. If you're not bleeding or unconscious, you go to work. 99

—Barney Blakeney, *Charleston (SC) City Paper.*

By the time Amy Robinson was 8 years old, she had already undergone 25 different surgeries. Born with congenital kidney disease, Robinson was in poor health, and her condition deteriorated further over the years. At the age of 21, when medications were costing her $1,400 per month, her kidneys began to fail. Two years later she entered the hospital and had a kidney transplant. Robinson had been working 3 jobs and was covered by private health insurance as well as supplemental coverage from the state. In spite of this, however, following her surgery she received bills for thousands of dollars, and the hospital would not allow her to stretch out payments over time. Drowning in debt, Robinson felt she had no choice but to declare bankruptcy. Today she works for a teaching union in Topeka, Kansas. She again has health insurance, but she still spends more than $500 per month on medications, physician visits, and laboratory work. Robinson finds life to be a constant struggle, and she continues to sink further and further into debt. "Every bit of money I spend is a decision," she says. "Even the McDonald's coffee I bought this morning. Every dime. I'm probably never going to get out of the hole. Even if the status quo holds with my kidney, all I am looking at is more medical bills."[19]

> Health care economists often refer to America's working poor as 'tweeners,' because in terms of health care they fall in between the poor, the wealthy, and the elderly.

The Plight of the Working Poor

Health care economists often refer to America's working poor as "tweeners," because in terms of health care they fall in between the poor, the wealthy, and the elderly. Many of them work at two or even three jobs. The wages that they earn may be barely enough to support their families, but their incomes are above the level that qualifies them for Medicaid. Unless they are disabled or over the age of 65, they do not qualify for Medicare. Health insurance is not an option because most of the working poor are either employed by companies that do not provide insurance to employees or charge premiums that are not affordable. As a result, if these people seek medical care, they must pay for the expenses out of pocket. When faced with the decision of whether to see a doctor, purchase prescription medicines, or pay the rent and buy groceries to feed their families, they must choose the latter. In a report published by the Commonwealth Fund in August 2008, the authors write: "The economic downturn is forcing working families across the United States to make tough financial choices, often involving sacrificing needed health care and health insurance."[20]

Studies have shown that one of the main types of health care that uninsured Americans forego is dental care. Parents who have sick children will undoubtedly find a way to get medical treatment for them, even if it means incurring the bills of an emergency room. But unless they have access to a free dental clinic, visits to the dentist are rare or nonexistent. Journalist Malcolm Gladwell writes:

> People without health insurance have bad teeth because, if you're paying for everything out of your own pocket, going to the dentist for a checkup seems like a luxury. It isn't, of course. The loss of teeth makes eating fresh fruits and vegetables difficult, and a diet heavy in soft, processed foods exacerbates more serious health problems, like diabetes. The pain of tooth decay leads many people to use alcohol as a salve. And those struggling to get ahead in the job market quickly find that the unsightliness of bad teeth, and the self-consciousness that results, can become a major barrier. [21]

Higher Prices for the Uninsured

A serious problem suffered by those who are uninsured is that they are often charged substantially more for medical services than people who have health coverage. This is because hospitals and medical providers set "official" charges (much like the maximum list price of a new automobile), which they agree to discount based on negotiations with insurance companies and government health plans. When they bill people who have no insurance, most providers do not offer the discount; instead, they bill at the highest possible rate. According to a study by Gerard F. Anderson, a health economist at the Johns Hopkins Bloomberg School of Public Health, uninsured patients who pay with their own money are charged 2.5 times more for hospital care than those who are insured, and more than 3 times the allowable amount covered by Medicare. He explains: "In the 1950s, the uninsured and poor were charged the lowest prices for medical service. Today they pay the highest prices, often two to three times more than what a person with health insurance would pay for hospital care."[22]

Rebekah Nix, a woman who moved from Midland, Texas, to New York City, experienced this disparity for herself. She had lost her job as a magazine fact-checker and was living on unemployment benefits of $1,122 per month. Because Medicaid's maximum income requirement for a single person was $352 per month, Nix did not qualify for coverage and had no private health insurance. In April 2002, after suffering from stabbing pains in her abdomen, she went to the emergency room at Brooklyn's New York Methodist Hospital. Tests confirmed that she had appendicitis and needed to have her appendix removed. To keep costs as low as possible Nix opted to have a laparoscopy, which required a shorter stay in the hospital, and she was released 42 hours later. In July she received a bill for $13,110—even though New York Methodist was typically paid $2,500 for the same procedure by health maintenance organizations (HMOs) and $5,000 by Medicare. In addition, Nix received separate invoices totaling $5,000 from the surgeon, the anesthesiologist, and other physicians who had treated her. With a monthly salary that barely covered her living expenses

> **A serious problem suffered by those who are uninsured is that they are often charged substantially more for medical services than people who have health coverage.**

and just $2,000 in her bank account, she could not afford to pay the bills. She wrote to the hospital, explaining that she was willing to make payments but the amount they were charging her was more money that she made in a year. When she received no response to her letter, Nix left New York and flew home to Texas. Someone notified the *Wall Street Journal* about her situation and a reporter contacted New York Methodist, which agreed to reduce Nix's debt to $5,000.

Illegal Billing

In many cases medical providers illegally bill patients through a practice known as "balance billing." This occurs when insurers pay physicians, laboratories, and/or hospitals their approved discounted rates, and patients are billed for the difference. According to *BusinessWeek*, which performed an investigation during 2008, balance billing is illegal in 47 states. In those states, if providers have agreed to participate in an insurance plan, they are bound by law not to attempt to collect the balance from the patient. Most people are not aware of this, however, and fearing that their credit will be tarnished, they go ahead and pay the bills. According to Jane Cooper, who is chief executive officer of a Milwaukee firm that helps people fight billing errors, some physicians, hospitals, and laboratories knowingly take advantage of consumer confusion. "Medical providers count on the fact that people will pay these bills because they don't have time to figure it out,"[23] she says.

> **In many cases, medical providers illegally bill patients through a practice known as 'balance billing.'**

BusinessWeek's investigative report cited one victim of balance billing, Yolanda Fil, who was insured by Horizon Blue Cross Blue Shield of New Jersey. After she had gall bladder surgery in 2005, Horizon paid bills that were submitted by the hospital, surgeon, and anesthesiologist but reduced its payment to the approved amount. In 2006 Fil received a bill from Vanguard Anesthesia Associates for $518, which the firm said she was responsible for because it was left over after insurance reimbursement. When Fil did not pay the bill, a collection agency began hounding her, and she eventually felt forced to pay it. "I didn't have any choice," she says. "They threatened me with bad credit."[24] An investigation by Horizon showed that Vanguard had billed 8,000 of its policyholders more than $4 million that had not been paid by insurance companies. Since New Jersey is one of the states where the practice is illegal, Horizon sued Vanguard in December 2006. A judge later ruled in favor of Horizon and ordered Vanguard to stop balance billing and to refund money to all patients who had paid.

Coverage for the Poor

Since 1965 low-income people in the United States have been eligible for health insurance coverage under Medicaid. Sometimes known as a safety net program, Medicaid has provided for millions of individuals and families who otherwise would not have access to health care. Although it is primarily run by the states, each Medicaid program must comply with national rules in order to obtain matching funding from the federal government. Each state has the authority to set its own individual guidelines—and according to an April 2007 report by the Public Citizen Health Research Group, this has led to marked disparities from state to state. One example of this disparity is the quality of care provided by medical facilities and nursing homes. With a maximum score of 200 points for quality, the top five states were Massachusetts (143), Rhode Island (109), Ohio (106.7), Florida (106.4), and Nebraska (105.4). These are in stark contrast to the 5 states that scored lowest in quality: Idaho (-4.4), Oklahoma (-3.8), Nevada (8.4), Louisiana (10.2), and Kansas (18.0). Comparable disparities from state to state were found in categories such as eligibility, scope of services, and provider reimbursement. "Overall, and in many ways," the report's authors conclude, "Medicaid is failing to deliver care to millions of people desperately in need of good quality health services."[25]

> **Jada needed a consultation with a rheumatology specialist, but she could find only one who was listed in her Medicaid plan's network, and he refused to see her in his office.**

Another challenge faced by those who have Medicaid coverage is that their choices of health care providers are extremely limited because growing numbers of physicians will not accept their insurance. This is, according to a report by the Health Research Group, because of "miserly reimbursement policies in many states." In an effort to balance their budgets, some Medicaid programs so deeply discount the amounts they pay that more and more providers are refusing to participate with the program. "In this important category," the report's authors write, "31 states had scores that were less than 50 percent of the total possible 250 points."[26] Another study by the Center for Studying Health System Change reported that nearly half of all doctors polled said they had either stopped accepting Medicaid altogether or were strictly limiting the number of new Medicaid patients. In Michigan, for example, an estimated 88 percent of doctors were willing to accept Medicaid in 1999. By 2005 the number had decreased to 64 percent and has continued to decline since then.

This has adversely affected many people who are covered by Medicaid, such as 16-year-old Jada Garrett from Benton Harbor, Michigan. In February 2007 she developed symptoms that initially seemed like a mild case of strep throat. Within a few weeks, however, her joints swelled up so badly that she was in too much pain to walk. Jada needed a consultation with a rheumatology specialist, but she could find only one who was listed in her Medicaid plan's network, and he refused to see her in his office. Two months passed before Jada found a rheumatologist in another county who was willing to see her, and by that time she was in such terrible pain that she had missed several weeks of school.

An Ongoing Struggle for the Uninsured

About 300 million people live in the United States, and an estimated 84 percent are covered by private health insurance, Medicare, or Medicaid. That means the majority of Americans have the comfort of knowing that all, or at least most, of their medical bills will be paid by either insurers or the government. But what about those who do not have such assurance? The working poor, the tweeners, are the ones who are left behind under the current health care system. Many work more than one job to make ends meet, but once their living expenses are paid, no money is left to pay insurance premiums—which means they have no choice but to forego medical and dental care for themselves and their families. Health executive Patricia H. White shares her thoughts about what these people face day to day: "All too often we close one eye to the reality of other people's lives. If it doesn't affect us, then it doesn't exist. [The working poor] live without life-sustaining medicine, put off going to the doctor, and choose between medicine and food because they simply can't afford it."[27] Those who vigorously support health care reform hope that this sort of inequity will soon become a thing of the past.

Primary Source Quotes*

Who Suffers Most Under the Current Health Care System?

66 **The most visible victims of America's decision to treat health care as a privilege are the 45 million Americans who lack insurance.** 99

—American Medical Student Association (AMSA), "The Case for Universal Health Care," 2006. www.amsa.org.

AMSA is a student-governed, national organization that is committed to representing the concerns of physicians-in-training.

66 **One prominent study places the total for the long-term uninsured as low as 8.2 million—a very different reality than the media and national health care advocates claim.** 99

—Julia A. Seymour, "Health Care Lie: '47 Million Uninsured Americans,'" Business & Media Institute, July 18, 2007. www.businessandmedia.org.

Seymour is assistant editor/analyst for the Business & Media Institute of the Media Research Center.

Bracketed quotes indicate conflicting positions.

* Editor's Note: While the definition of a primary source can be narrowly or broadly defined, for the purposes of Compact Research, a primary source consists of: 1) results of original research presented by an organization or researcher; 2) eyewitness accounts of events, personal experience, or work experience; 3) first-person editorials offering pundits' opinions; 4) government officials presenting political plans and/or policies; 5) representatives of organizations presenting testimony or policy.

66 The lives of the working poor are . . . harder because the safety net is fraying. As workers inch up the pay scale, government and private aid for child care, health care and rent begins to fall away, and they actually can wind up with less money in their pockets than the region's poorest residents. 99

—Carol Smith and Paul Nyhan, "Surprising Face of Working Poor," *Seattle Post-Intelligencer*, February 16, 2006. http://seattlepi.nwsource.com.

Smith and Nyhan are reporters for the *Seattle Post-Intelligencer* newspaper.

66 We provide large public subsidies to the elderly, to the very poor, and even to workers with good jobs— through the tax exclusion for employer-based health plans. But a great many Americans, 45 million by the conventional way of counting, don't fit into any of these boxes and so lack insurance coverage for their health care. 99

—Sidney Taurel, "The Critical Condition: The Ills of America's Health Care System, and How We Can Heal Them," Remarks to the World Health Care Congress, February 1, 2005. www.lilly.com.

Taurel is chairman and chief executive officer of Eli Lilly and Company.

66 Poverty's impact is felt most by the nation's children. Children under the age of 5 are more likely to live in extreme poverty. Uninsured children are at greater risk of experiencing health problems such as obesity, heart disease and asthma that continue to affect them later in adulthood. 99

—Sabriya Rice, "Poverty and Health Are Intertwined, Experts Say," CNN *Health*, September 4, 2006. www.cnn.com.

Rice is an associate producer with the CNN Medical Unit.

> **"As a whole, the uninsured have more chronic illnesses and are sicker than those with insurance, because they receive no preventative health care services and disease prevention education."**

—Laurie Anderson, "The Time Has Come: Universal Health Insurance," WebMD, August 17, 2007. http://blogs.webmd.com.

Anderson is a family nurse practitioner in a rural health care clinic that serves Native Americans.

> **"How long you live should not depend on how rich you are. But recent studies show that the richer you are, the longer you live."**

—Donald Warne, "Native American Health Suffers Due to Inequality," *Progressive*, May 20, 2008. www.progressive.org.

Warne is president and CEO of American Indian Health Management & Policy in Phoenix, Arizona.

> **"Those without health insurance face sky-high doctor and hospital bills and ever more aggressive collection tactics—when they receive care at all."**

—Joel A. Harrison, "Paying More, Getting Less: Just Where Do America's Health Care Dollars Go?" *Dollars and Sense*, May/June, 2008. www.dollarsandsense.org.

Harrison is a health care consultant from San Diego.

> **"In 2006, 14.8 percent of Americans, or 43.6 million, were currently without health insurance."**

—Centers for Disease Control and Prevention (CDC), "Uninsured Americans: Newly Released Health Insurance Statistics," August 8, 2007. www.cdc.gov.

The CDC is charged with promoting health and quality of life by controlling disease, injury, and disability.

66 From 1990 to 2005, the Medicaid caseload doubled to 55 million participants, meaning that the government is increasingly taking over the health care system from private companies, community, and charitable organizations, thus eroding self-reliance, independence, and local community responsibilities. 99

—Brian M. Riedl, "The Myths of Spending Cuts for the Poor, Tax Cuts for the Rich," Heritage Foundation, February 14, 2006. www.heritage.org.

Riedl is Grover M. Hermann Fellow in Federal Budgetary Affairs in the Thomas A. Roe Institute for Economic Policy Studies at the Heritage Foundation.

66 The world's richest health care system is unable to assure such basics as prenatal care and immunizations, and we trail most of the developed world on such indicators as infant mortality and life expectancy. 99

—Physicians for a National Health Program (PNHP), "Proposal of the Physicians' Working Group for Single-Payer National Health Insurance," 2008. www.pnhp.org.

PNHP is an organization that advocates a universal, comprehensive single-payer national health program.

66 A coroner's report will never list lack of insurance as a cause of death, but people in fact die when they do not have access to appropriate care. 99

—David B. Kendall, "Fixing America's Health Care System," Progressive Policy Institute (PPI) *Policy Report*, September 2005. www.ppionline.org.

Kendall is PPI's senior fellow for health policy.

Facts and Illustrations

Who Suffers Most Under the Current Health Care System?

- The U.S. Census Bureau reports that the number of uninsured Americans rose from **31 million** in 1987 to nearly **46 million in 2007**.

- According to the Commonwealth Fund, nearly **9 million people** in the United States have lost their health insurance since 2000.

- During 2008, **$490 billion**, collected from American taxpayers, was spent on funding Medicare and Medicaid.

- The American College of Physicians reports that the percentage of people with government insurance, including Medicare, Medicaid, and military health care, increased from **24.7 percent** in 2000 to **27 percent** in 2006.

- An estimated **50 percent** of bankruptcies in the United States are the result of unpaid medical bills.

- A study published in *Health Affairs* in 2008 showed that U.S. hospitals charged patients without health insurance an average of **2.5 times** more for services than fees paid by health insurers and **3 times** more than Medicare.

- The Kaiser Family Foundation states that eligibility standards for Medicaid and SCHIP **do not keep pace** with rapid increases in health care costs.

Diminishing Access to Health Care

As health costs have continued to soar, growing numbers of people in the United States have lost their health insurance and therefore have little or no access to medical care. The U.S. Census Bureau reports that in 2007, an estimated 46 million Americans were uninsured. These maps show a state-by-state breakdown of how the number of uninsured has grown since 2000.

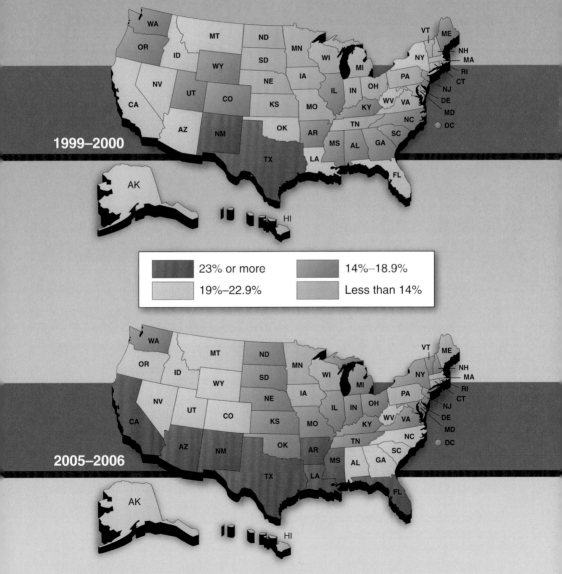

1999–2000

23% or more	14%–18.9%
19%–22.9%	Less than 14%

2005–2006

Source: Commonwealth Fund, "Why Not the Best?" July 2008. www.commonwealthfund.org.

Perspectives on the U.S. Health Care System

The American Federation of Labor and Congress of Industrial Organizations (AFL-CIO) is a voluntary federation of 56 national and international labor unions. During a January–March 2008 survey by the AFL-CIO the majority of more than 26,000 participants said that they have major concerns about America's heath care system, and many fear for their future.

Overall, what do you think about today's health care system?

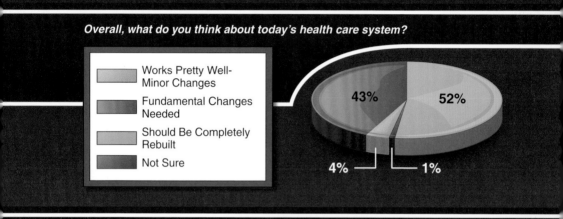

- Works Pretty Well- Minor Changes
- Fundamental Changes Needed
- Should Be Completely Rebuilt
- Not Sure

43% 52% 4% 1%

Looking ahead over the next few years, are you concerned about affording health insurance?

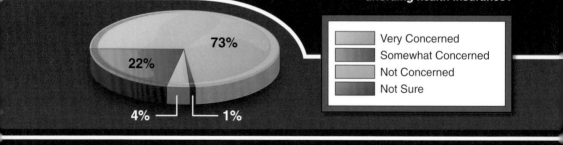

- Very Concerned
- Somewhat Concerned
- Not Concerned
- Not Sure

73% 22% 4% 1%

Are you concerned about losing health coverage because you may lose your job or change jobs?

- Very Concerned
- Somewhat Concerned
- Not Concerned
- Not Sure

46% 4% 26% 24%

Source: AFL-CIO "2008 Health Care for America Survey," March 2008. www.aflcio.org.

Who Suffers Most Under America's Health Care System?

Burdened by Medical Costs

Although the majority of Americans have some health insurance, either from private or public sources, millions of people are struggling because of medical bills and debt.

An Estimated 116 Million Adults Were Uninsured, Underinsured, Reported a Medical Bill Problem, and/or Did Not Access Needed Health Care Because of Cost in 2007

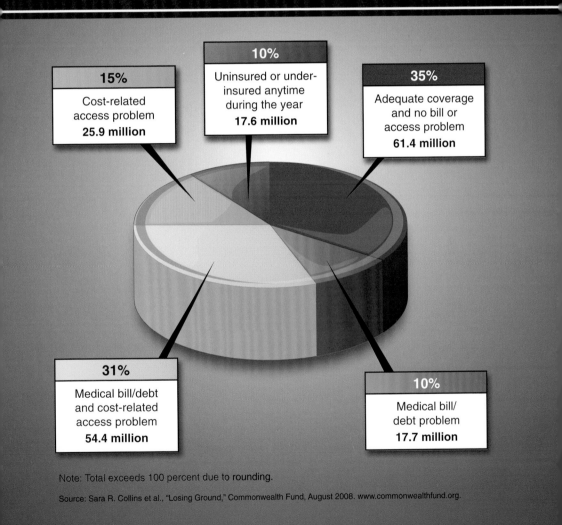

15%
Cost-related access problem
25.9 million

10%
Uninsured or under-insured anytime during the year
17.6 million

35%
Adequate coverage and no bill or access problem
61.4 million

31%
Medical bill/debt and cost-related access problem
54.4 million

10%
Medical bill/ debt problem
17.7 million

Note: Total exceeds 100 percent due to rounding.

Source: Sara R. Collins et al., "Losing Ground," Commonwealth Fund, August 2008. www.commonwealthfund.org.

The Working Poor

Tens of millions of adults in the United States work at one or more jobs, but still cannot afford to pay for health insurance or medical care because they only make enough money to pay for basic living expenses. A July 2008 survey of low-wage workers revealed how serious a problem health care is for the working poor.

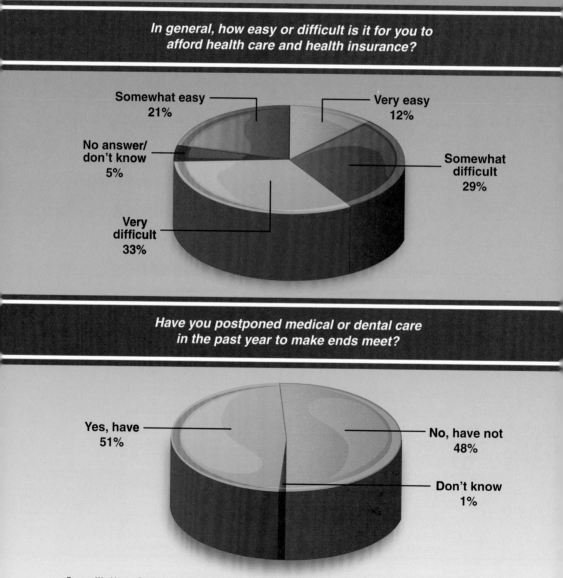

In general, how easy or difficult is it for you to afford health care and health insurance?

Somewhat easy — 21%

Very easy — 12%

No answer/ don't know — 5%

Somewhat difficult — 29%

Very difficult — 33%

Have you postponed medical or dental care in the past year to make ends meet?

Yes, have — 51%

No, have not — 48%

Don't know — 1%

Source: *Washington Post*/Kaiser Family Foundation/Harvard University, "Survey of Low-Wage Workers," August 4, 2008. www.kff.org.

- According to the American Cancer Society, the uninsured are **60 percent** more likely than insured patients to die within five years of being diagnosed.

- The National Coalition on Health Care states that nearly **25 percent** of the uninsured report making significant changes in their way of life in order to pay medical bills.

- The Commonwealth Fund states that between 2001 and 2007 the share of adults who reported problems getting needed health care because of costs rose from 29 to **45 percent.**

- A joint survey in 2007 by the *Wall Street Journal* and NBC News showed that nearly **50 percent** of Americans say that the cost of health care is their **number one economic concern.**

- According to the CDC, **10 percent of women** aged 45 to 64 whose income was below the poverty level delayed medical care due to a lack of transportation.

- The CDC states that about **33 percent of all children** living below the poverty level did not have a recent dental visit in 2005, compared with less than **20 percent** of higher-income children.

- Those who lack insurance often visit hospital emergency rooms for **nonemergency conditions**; studies show that the number of ER visits has increased **20 percent** over the past 10 years.

- The Commonwealth Fund reports that more than **70 percent** of adults with gaps in their health insurance coverage reported not getting needed health care because of cost—up from just over half in 2001.

Should America's Health Care Be Nationalized?

66The cause of the U.S. health-care mess is governmental interference. The solution, therefore, is not more governmental control, whether via nationalized medical insurance or a government takeover of medicine.99

—Onkar Ghate, *BusinessWeek.*

66Our government's responsibility is to guarantee quality affordable health care for everyone in America and it must play a central role in regulating, financing, and providing health coverage.99

—Healthcare for America NOW! "Statement of Common Purpose."

On October 13, 2004, George W. Bush participated in a debate with presidential candidate John Kerry. After Bush was asked by the moderator to comment on health care in the United States, he responded that some type of solution was certainly in order, but nationalized health care was not the answer. "I think government-run health will lead to poor-quality health, will lead to rationing, will lead to less choice," he said.

Once a health-care program ends up in a line item in the federal government budget, it leads to more controls.

And just look at other countries that have tried to have federally controlled health care. They have poor-quality health care. Our health-care system is the envy of the world because we believe in making sure that the decisions are made by doctors and patients, not by officials in the nation's capital.[28]

Americans are deeply divided on the issue of nationalized health care. People who agree with Bush are convinced that the federal government has no business running the health care system and that putting the government in control would create additional bureaucracy and result in lower health care quality. Those who disagree believe it is the government's responsibility to ensure health care for every man, woman, and child in the United States.

What Is Nationalized Health Care?

When people talk about health care, the terms "nationalized" and "universal" are often used interchangeably. Karen Ignagni, president and CEO of the trade group America's Health Insurance Plans, explains: "There's an assumption (in the public) that universal coverage means government-run."[29] The two are not the same, however. Under a universal system, all citizens have access to health care, but the system is not necessarily controlled by the government. With a nationalized system, such as the one in the United Kingdom, the government is in control and is responsible for providing and paying for health care with tax dollars. People who live in the United Kingdom pay taxes that are earmarked for health care, and the government-run National Health Service distributes the funds to health care providers. Doctors who work for hospitals are paid salaries, while general practitioners who run private practices are paid based on the number of patients they see. For most medical services no copayments are required,

> " Under a universal system, all citizens have access to health care, but the system is not necessarily controlled by the government. "

although some copayments are required for dental care, eyeglasses, and prescription medicines. Young people and the elderly do not have to make copayments for drugs.

Those who are critical of nationalized systems say that when the government is in control, the inevitable result is health care rationing. As Stossel and Sullivan write: "If it's decided that health care should be paid for with tax dollars, then it's up to the government to decide how that money should be spent. . . . When health care is free, governments deal with all that increased demand by limiting what's available." John Stossel and Andrew Sullivan add that another problem with nationalized health care is long waiting times for patients. "The reality of 'free' health care is that people wait. In the United Kingdom, one in eight patients waits more than a year for hospital treatment. . . . In Canada, almost a million citizens are waiting for necessary surgery and more than a million Canadians can't find a regular doctor."[30]

> **Another criticism of nationalized health care is that the government pressures medical providers and hospitals to keep costs low, which can take a heavy toll on quality.**

Another criticism of nationalized health care is that the government pressures medical providers and hospitals to keep costs low, which can take a heavy toll on quality. When David Asman's wife was hospitalized in England, only one person was responsible for cleaning the entire hospital, and Asman found the hospital to be dirty and unsanitary. Because he worried about germs, he frequently cleaned his wife's room himself. He says it was a blessing that her bed was near a window because "the smells wafting through the ward were often overwhelming." Asman also noted that the medical equipment was old and outdated. "On occasion," he writes, "my wife and I would giggle at heart and blood-pressure monitors that were literally taped together and would come apart as they were being moved into place. The nurses and hospital technicians had become expert at jerry-rigging temporary fixes for a lot of the damaged equipment." According to Asman, hospital-borne infections are rampant in Great Britain, as he explains: "At least 100,000 British patients a year are hit by hospital-acquired infections, including the penicillin-resistant 'superbug' MRSA. A new study carried out by the British Health Protection Agency says that MRSA plays a part in the deaths of up to 32,000 patients every year. But even at lower numbers, Britain has the worst MRSA infection rates in Europe. It's not hard to see why."[31]

Health Care in Germany

Many who advocate universal health care use Germany as an example, saying that the country has one of the best health care systems in the world. Unlike in the United States, everyone in Germany has equal access to quality health care, as National Public Radio health correspondent Richard Knox explains: "Germans really hate any hint of unfairness in health care. The fundamental idea is that everybody must be covered and, preferably, everybody should get equal treatment."[32] The German government does not control the health care system but rather acts as a referee, making sure that it remains fair and affordable for everyone. It revolves around more than 200 nonprofit insurance companies known as "sickness funds" that reimburse patients for medical care and which people choose based on their personal preference. The individual sickness funds compete against each other for members, and managers are motivated to grow their funds because they are paid based on the size of their enrollment. Each year they negotiate with their doctors and hospitals to determine the annual budget. The government closely regulates all activity to ensure that premiums are kept at a reasonable level and are not raised for reasons such as advancing age or chronic illness. Yet even though Germany's system provides health care for nearly all of its citizens, the country's average per capita cost is about half of what the United States spends. Its percentage of health spending as part of gross domestic product is less than 11 percent, compared to America's 16 percent.

Financing of Germany's health care system is largely through income tax. All workers are required to pay about 8 percent of their gross income into their sickness fund, which means that people with low incomes naturally pay less than higher-income individuals. Employers contribute another 8 percent for each worker. Those who are poor or unable to work receive government assistance to pay for health care. The only people who may not participate in the program are those who are self-employed; they must purchase their own coverage from private insurers, but their families are covered by the sickness fund.

The health benefits under the German system are very generous, covering all medical expenses, diagnostic tests, hospitalization, and prescription drugs, as well as dental, mental health, and optical care. There are no deductibles, no rationing of care, and no exempting people for reasons such as preexisting conditions. Jan and Sabina Casagrandes live in the German city of Cologne, and they are extremely happy with the country's health care system. When Sabina was 33 years old, she developed a huge tumor on her neck, which tests showed to be malignant. She underwent two operations to have the tumor removed and then had radiation treatments following the surgery. Now cancer-free, she says that she could not imagine better health care than she received, and it went beyond just medical expenses. While she was recovering at home she was physically unable to care for her daughter, so her insurer paid for a friend to do the shopping and cooking and to help care for the baby. According to Knox, that is not unusual in Germany. "In fact," he says, "under the country's system for long-term care, family members can choose to be paid for taking care of a frail elder at home if they want to avoid nursing home care."[33]

> "Although Germany's health care system is not without its flaws, it is superior to that of the United States."

Health economist Karl Lauterbach says that although Germany's health care system is not without its flaws, it is superior to that of the United States. He explains: "In comparison to the U.S. health care system, the German system is clearly better, because the German health care system works for everyone who needs care, . . . [costs] little money, and it's not a system about which you have to worry all the time. So in case you need health care, the health care is there. That you can rely on." Lauterbach points out one of the biggest problems of America's health care system: "The [Americans] who are insured do have to worry whether they are able to pay the bills. People become bankrupt because they cannot pay the medical bills, and there are vast differences in the quality of care depending on how much you are prepared and able to pay. I think the system is not working well."[34]

The Dutch System

Like Germany, the Netherlands has a universal health care system. It was implemented in January 2006 with the passage of the Health Insurance Act, the culmination of years of legislation and policies that attempted to achieve universal health coverage for all Dutch citizens. Today, everyone who lives or works in the Netherlands has access to health care. Workers pay a percentage of annual income to a tax collector who deposits the contributions in a Risk Equalization Fund (REF), and employers are legally bound to compensate employees for the health care taxes that they pay. Every adult in the Netherlands can choose his or her preferred private insurance company, and no one can be rejected because of preexisting medical conditions.

In addition to the health care income tax, people in the Netherlands pay a premium directly to their chosen insurer. The system emphasizes value and competition—the Dutch government has developed a Web site that allows consumers to compare all insurers in terms of price, services, and consumer satisfaction, as well as to compare hospitals on various sets of performance indicators. In 2008 the average insurance premium was about $1,600 per adult per year. No premiums are charged for coverage of children under the age of 18; the government reimburses the REF for their health care costs. To compensate for the cost of health insurance premiums, the government allocates subsidies, known as care allowances, to the majority of Dutch households at a maximum of $2,200 per household per year.

> " According to a March–May 2007 survey by Harris Interactive, the Dutch rate their health care system higher than do people living in Spain, Canada, France, Great Britain, Germany, New Zealand, Australia, Italy, and the United States. "

According to a March–May 2007 survey by Harris Interactive, the Dutch rate their health care system higher than do people living in Spain, Canada, France, Great Britain, Germany, New Zealand, Australia, Italy, and the United States. When 1,000 adults from each of those countries were asked if their system works "pretty well with only minor changes needed," the Netherlands was rated the most popular at 42 percent while the United States scored only 12 percent. When asked if the health care system should be completely rebuilt, the Netherlands again scored the highest with only 9 percent saying yes. In contrast, 33 percent of Americans said that so much was wrong with the health care system that it needed to be rebuilt, and 50 percent of respondents said that "fundamental changes are needed to make it work better."[35]

Unknown Outcome

Nationalized health care is a contentious issue in the United States. Even many who acknowledge that America's current system is sorely in need of reform denounce the idea of more government involvement, saying that nationalized programs in other countries are inferior to health care in the United States. Those who advocate nationalization believe that it is the only fair and equitable type of system and that it is the government's responsibility to ensure health care for all its citizens. Robert J. Kuttner, who is a senior fellow at a public policy research and advocacy organization in New York, shares his thoughts: "Sometimes, we Americans do the right thing only after having exhausted all other alternatives. It remains to be seen how much exhaustion the health care system will suffer before we turn to national health insurance."[36]

Primary Source Quotes*

Should America's Health Care Be Nationalized?

> **The answer . . . to America's health care problems lies not in heading down the road to national health care but in learning from the experiences of other countries, which demonstrate the failure of centralized command and control and the benefits of increasing consumer incentives and choice.**

—Michael D. Tanner, "The Grass Is Not Always Greener: A Look at National Health Care Systems Around the World," Cato Institute *Policy Analysis*, March 18, 2008. www.cato.org.

Tanner is director of health and welfare studies for the libertarian think tank Cato Institute.

> **We need true universal health care reform that covers every single man, woman, and child in America. It is wrong to leave anyone without the care they need. A universal system will work better for all of us—delivering better care at lower cost.**

—John Edwards, "Edwards Statements on Health Care Mandate," news release, 2008. www.johnedwards.com.

Edwards is a former Democratic senator from North Carolina.

Bracketed quotes indicate conflicting positions.

* Editor's Note: While the definition of a primary source can be narrowly or broadly defined, for the purposes of Compact Research, a primary source consists of: 1) results of original research presented by an organization or researcher; 2) eyewitness accounts of events, personal experience, or work experience; 3) first-person editorials offering pundits' opinions; 4) government officials presenting political plans and/or policies; 5) representatives of organizations presenting testimony or policy.

> **Contrary to claims that government-imposed 'universal health care' would solve America's health care problems, it would in fact destroy American medicine and countless lives along with it. The goal of 'universal health care' (a euphemism for socialized medicine) is both immoral and impractical.**

—Lin Zinser and Paul Hsieh, "Moral Health Care vs. 'Universal' Health Care," *Objective Standard*, Winter 2007–2008. www.theobjectivestandard.com.

Zinser is the founder of Freedom and Individual Rights in Medicine (FIRM); Hsieh is a physician from Denver, Colorado, and a founding member of FIRM.

> **Universal health care for every single American must not be a question of whether, it must be a question of how. We have the ideas, we have the resources, and we will have universal health care in this country by the end of the next president's first term.**

—Barack Obama, "The Time Has Come for Universal Health Care," January 25, 2007. http://obama.senate.gov.

Obama is a U.S. senator from Illinois and the 2008 Democratic nominee for president..

> **In addition to paying less, Canadians get more comprehensive care and have better health care outcomes.**

—Suzanne King, "Exercise Our Right to Better Health Care," Physicians for a National Health Program blog, August 11, 2008. www.pnhp.org.

King is a child and adolescent psychiatrist in Lenox, Massachusetts.

> **If you want to sell Americans on universal health coverage, it's not helpful to use a model that makes patients wait five weeks to see a cancer doctor. That's Canada.**

—Froma Harrop, "Canada's the Wrong Model for Universal Health Care," *Seattle Times*, February 28, 2007. http://seattletimes.nwsource.com.

Harrop is a syndicated columnist with the *Providence (RI) Journal* newspaper.

"While 'universal health care' may provide health insurance, it doesn't guarantee health care. The uninsured are not the problem but instead are a symptom of the real problem: Government meddling in personal choices over how we care for ourselves and our families."

—Brian Schwartz, "Universal Health Care Is the Wrong Prescription," *Health Care News*, June 1, 2008. www.heartland.org.

Schwartz is a writer who focuses on issues related to health care.

"A major culprit in the inconsistent performance of the nation's health system is that we fail to provide health insurance to nearly 45 million people and inadequately insure an additional 16 million more. Universal coverage is essential to placing the system on a path to high performance."

—Sara R. Collins, "Universal Health Insurance: Why It Is Essential to Achieving a High Performance Health System and Why Design Matters," congressional testimony, June 26, 2007. www.commonwealthfund.org.

Collins is assistant vice president of the Commonwealth Fund.

"America spends more than twice as much per capita on health care as France, and almost two and a half times as much as Britain. But it falls down in almost every key indicator of health, starting, perhaps, most shockingly, with infant mortality—36 percent higher than in Britain."

—Andrew Gumbel, "Surviving the U.S. Health Care System," *Seattle Post-Intelligencer*, June 29, 2007. http://seattlepi.nwsource.com.

Gumbel is an American correspondent for the *Independent*, a British newspaper.

"I think we have all learned that America needs to provide health insurance for all Americans."

—Hillary Rodham Clinton, "Health Care: Remarks on American Health Choices Plan," September 17, 2007. www.hillaryclinton.com.

Clinton is a Democratic senator from New York.

“Taken as a whole, Britain's universal healthcare system has evolved into a ramshackle structure where tests are underperformed, equipment is undersupplied, operations are underdone, and medical personnel are overworked, underpaid and overly tied down in red tape.”

—Ralph R. Reiland, "Healthcare to Die for in Britain?" *Capitalism Magazine*, February 26, 2005. www.capmag.com.

Reiland is the B. Kenneth Simon Professor of Free Enterprise at Robert Morris University in Pittsburgh, Pennsylvania.

“An expanded and improved Medicare for All . . . program would cover everyone comprehensively within our current expenditures and eliminate the need for private insurance. This is the direction we must go.”

—Leonard Rodberg and Don McCanne, "Health Insurance for the 21st Century," Physicians for a National Health Program (PNHP), July 13, 2007. www.pnhp.org.

Rodberg is research director of the New York Metro Chapter of PNHP, and McCanne is senior policy fellow at PNHP.

“The current Medicare system is ineffective at reducing health care costs. Indeed, it is a major cause of the escalation of such costs. There is no reason to think that Medicare for All would be any different.”

—David Hogberg, "'Medicare for All' Universal Health Care Would Not Solve the Problem of Rising Health Care Costs," *National Policy Analysis*, September 2007. www.nationalcenter.org.

Hogberg is a health care policy expert and former senior fellow and senior policy analyst at the National Center for Public Policy Research.

“Health care costs will increase and quality decrease with every increase in government involvement.”

—Charles L. Armstrong, "The Politics of American Healthcare," Lew Rockwell, February 22, 2005. www.lewrockwell.com.

Armstrong is a physician from Oxnard, California.

Should America's Health Care Be Nationalized?

- Compared with America's health care spending of **16 percent** of the GDP, in 2007, Germany spent **9.7 percent** and Canada and France each spent **9.5 percent**.

- A 2007 study by the Commonwealth Fund showed that in terms of quality of care, equity of care, access to care, efficiencies, and health outcomes, the United States **scored last out of five industrialized countries**.

- McKinsey Global Institute reported in January 2007 that the United States spends **six times more per capita** on health care administration than Western European countries.

- According to the Commonwealth Fund, **46 percent** of sick Americans can get an appointment with a doctor on the same or next day compared with New Zealand (74 percent), the Netherlands (69 percent), Germany (63 percent), Australia (58 percent), and the United Kingdom (57 percent). Only Canada scored lower than the United States.

- Americans' life expectancy at birth is **77.9 years** compared with people in Japan (82 years), Singapore (81.8 years), France (80.6 years), Sweden (80.6 years), Australia (80.6 years), Switzerland (80.6 years), and Canada (80.3 years).

Americans Support Nationalized Health Care

According to a November 2007 Gallup poll, the majority of people in the United States support a national health care system.

Do you think it is the responsibility of the federal government to make sure all Americans have health care coverage, or is that not the responsibility of the federal government?

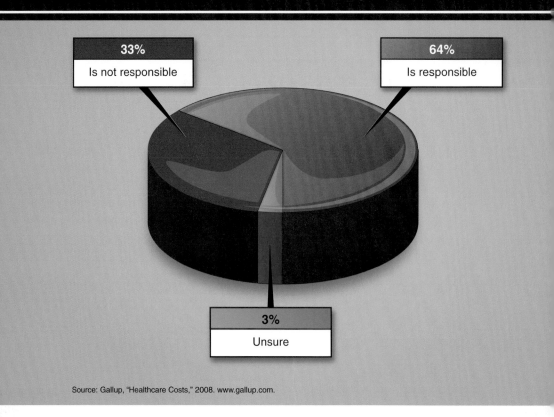

33%
Is not responsible

64%
Is responsible

3%
Unsure

Source: Gallup, "Healthcare Costs," 2008. www.gallup.com.

- Surveys have shown that the number one reason the uninsured do not have health insurance is that they **cannot afford the premiums**.

- According to the American Medical Association (AMA), about **18,000 people** in the United States die each year because they do not have health coverage.

- According to the United Health Foundation, the prevalence of many major chronic diseases (such as heart disease, high blood pressure, stroke, diabetes, lung disease, arthritis, and cancer) among adults aged 50 and older is **higher in the United States** compared with 10 European countries.

Health Care Satisfaction in Developed Nations

The United States is the only industrialized country in the world that does not have a system in place to provide health care for all its citizens. According to Harris Interactive surveys completed in 2007 and 2008, the Dutch are happiest with their health care, while Americans do not feel nearly as positive about theirs.

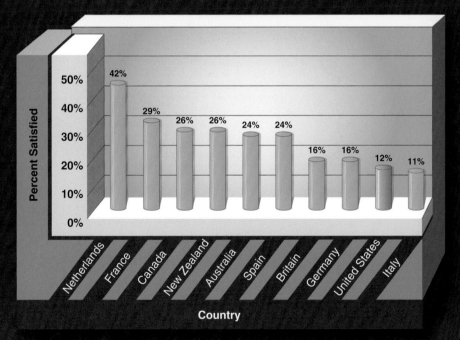

Source: Harris Interactive, "Health Care Systems in Ten Developed Countries: The U.S. System Is Most Unpopular and Dutch System the Most Popular," July 2, 2008. www.harrisinteractive.com.

U.S. Life Expectancy and IMR Below Many Modern Nations

One reason many Americans are against government-provided health care is their opinion that health care in the United States is superior to other countries'—but research shows that is not necessarily the case. Compared with several other industrialized nations, each of which has some form of universal health care, the United States has a lower overall life expectancy and a higher infant mortality rate.

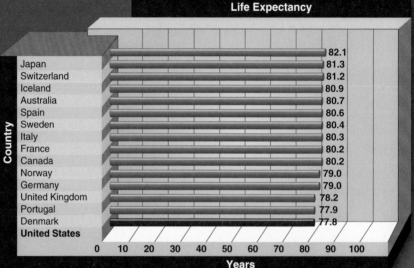

Life Expectancy

Country	Years
Japan	82.1
Switzerland	81.3
Iceland	81.2
Australia	80.9
Spain	80.7
Sweden	80.6
Italy	80.4
France	80.3
Canada	80.2
Norway	80.2
Germany	79.0
United Kingdom	79.0
Portugal	78.2
Denmark	77.9
United States	77.8

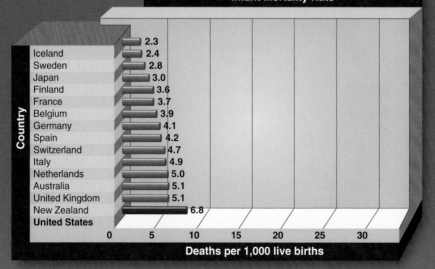

Infant Mortality Rate

Country	Deaths per 1,000 live births
Iceland	2.3
Sweden	2.4
Japan	2.8
Finland	3.0
France	3.6
Belgium	3.7
Germany	3.9
Spain	4.1
Switzerland	4.2
Italy	4.7
Netherlands	4.9
Australia	5.0
United Kingdom	5.1
New Zealand	5.1
United States	6.8

Source: Organisation for Economic Co-Operation and Development (OECD), "Health at a Glance 2007: OECD Indicators," November 13, 2007. http://oberon.sourceoecd.org.

Health Care Timeliness: A Global Comparison

Nationalized health care is a contentious issue in the United States, with many arguing that countries that have such systems are plagued with problems such as long waiting times and the inability to receive medical care on nights, weekends, and holidays. According to the Commonwealth Fund, however, these problems are worse in the United States than several other developed nations.

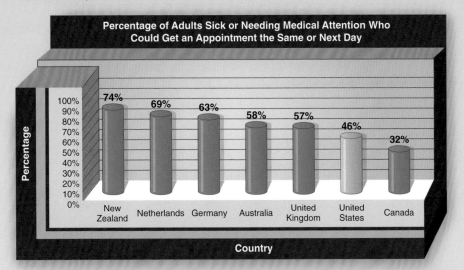

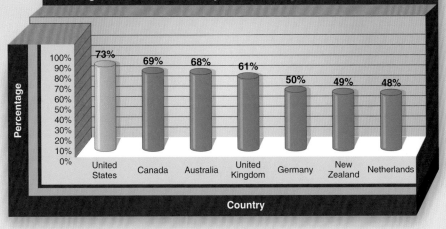

Source: Commonwealth Fund, "Why Not the Best?" July 2008. www.commonwealthfund.org.

- The AMA states that uninsured children are at least **70 percent** more likely to go without care for common childhood conditions, and more than 3 times as likely to go without needed prescription drugs.

- Economists estimate that between **25 and 45 percent** of the labor force in the United States is "job-locked," meaning that employees make career decisions based on their need to maintain health insurance coverage or to avoid being excluded because of a preexisting condition.

- The National Coalition on Health Care reports that the United States has **$480 billion** in excess health care spending each year compared with Western European countries that have universal health insurance.

- According to government analyst Robert Longley, **nationalized health insurance** would reduce the cost of American-made consumer products, which in turn would help U.S. companies be more competitive in global trade.

- A February 2006 American Consumer Institute survey showed that **43 percent** of people in the United States favor nationalized health care, compared with **50 percent** who oppose it.

- A report published in the May 3, 2006, issue of the *Journal of the American Medical Association* states that the American population in later middle age is **less healthy** than the equivalent British population for diabetes, hypertension, heart disease, myocardial infarction, stroke, lung disease, and cancer.

How Can America Improve Its Health Care System?

> **The American health care 'crisis' is not acute illness—rather it is like a chronic disease which flares up periodically, accompanied by fresh prophecies of impending doom and calls for someone on a white horse to fix the problem.**
>
> —Jeff Goldsmith, "The Perpetual Health Care Crisis."

> **The health care crisis is a national crisis and demands a national solution.**
>
> —United Food and Commercial Workers (UFCW), "Health Care Crisis."

In their best-selling book *Redefining Health Care*, authors Michael E. Porter and Elizabeth Olmsted Teisberg offer a frank opinion about the health care system in the United States. Their assessment is that America's health care is on "a collision course with patient needs and economic reality," and they sternly warn that if significant changes are not made, the enormity of the problem is certain to grow worse. Porter and Teisberg insist that the health care system today, with its soaring costs, deteriorating quality, and increasing numbers of people without health insurance, is "unacceptable and unsustainable."[37]

Without a radical approach to reforming the health care system so that a completely new and better structure is created, Porter and Teisberg predict that arbitrary budget cuts, price controls, and health care rationing, will be inevitable. Yet in spite of these dire predictions, they remain optimistic that a better outcome is possible. "The future of health care is not predetermined," they write. "Effective leaders have the insight to revisit the fundamental purpose of an organization and imagine a different and more effective way to attain it."[38] Although political leaders may, and often do, vehemently disagree on what is the best approach for reforming the health care system in the United States, with health care garnering such a large amount of attention, some type of reform is inevitable in the coming years. And that, say health care policy experts, is good news for America.

The Bush Administration Proposal

In his January 2007 State of the Union speech, George W. Bush unveiled his solution to the United States' ailing health care system. In an effort to make health insurance more affordable for the tens of millions of Americans who are uninsured, Bush suggested a proposal that revolved around tax deductions. Under his plan, families would be able to deduct $15,000 per year of their taxable income to help offset the cost of purchasing health insurance policies, and individuals would be eligible for a $7,500 annual tax deduction. Bush explained the benefits of such a plan:

> With this reform, more than 100 million men, women, and children who are now covered by employer-provided insurance will benefit from lower tax bills. At the same time, this reform will level the playing field for those who do not get health insurance through their job. For Americans who now purchase health insurance on their own, this proposal would mean a substantial tax savings—$4,500 for a family of four making $60,000 a year. And for the millions of other Americans who have no health insurance at all, this deduction would help put a basic private health insurance plan within their reach.[39]

Advocates of such a program lauded Bush's plan, saying that in addition to making health insurance affordable for many Americans who cannot purchase it now, the plan would help keep costs under control because people would be motivated to shop for the best value for their health care dollar. This, they say, is preferable to any sort of nationalized plan because people would be able to make their own decisions about health insurance, rather than the government making those decisions for them.

Critics of Bush's proposal argue that it is the wrong approach for American health care reform. Their main reasoning is that wealthier individuals and families would benefit far more than those with lower incomes. Because of the way the current tax system is structured, low-income families would receive such a small tax break that it would fall far short of generating enough money for them to pay for health insurance premiums. For example, a $15,000 deduction for a family taxed at the 35 percent rate would be worth about $5,250, while for those in the 10 percent bracket it would only be worth about $1,500. According to the ACHP Center for Policy and Research, the average annual cost of health insurance for a family ranges from $4,600 to more than $9,000 per year and varies widely from state to state. In Alaska, for example, 17 percent of the state's population is uninsured, and family health insurance policies cost as much as $13,700 per year, whereas in North Dakota a comparable family policy would be about $7,300. Obviously, $1,500 in annual tax savings—or even double that amount—would make little difference for the millions of Americans who are currently uninsured, and the expense of health insurance would remain beyond their financial means. "The president's proposals are an opportunity missed," says Senator Edward Kennedy. "They will not improve access to good coverage and won't help working families afford the spiraling cost of health care."[40]

> " In an effort to make health insurance more affordable for the tens of millions of Americans who are uninsured, Bush suggested a proposal that revolved around tax deductions. "

Consumer-Driven Health Care

Growing numbers of policy experts say that America's health care system is failing because an essential factor is missing from the equation:

competition. The many Americans with comprehensive health insurance have no reason to seek out the best value for their health care dollar because the insurers are footing the bills. Patients often have no idea whatsoever about the actual cost of medical care or diagnostic tests or hospitalization, or even prescription medicines. Harvard business professor and health care analyst Regina Herzlinger explains: "One of the key success factors of the U.S. economy is transparency. We know the prices and quality of the goods and services we buy, ranging from our morning cereal to our complex computers to our mutual funds. This transparency has enabled us to be smart shoppers. . . . That is why just about everybody supports transparency in all aspects of our lives—except health care."[41] Herzlinger believes that a consumer-driven system is the only viable option for true health care reform. Such a system would involve taking the money that employers and the government now receive from people via taxes and salaries, and putting it back into the hands of the American citizens so they can make intelligent comparisons and purchase their own insurance based on their personal preferences.

> **With the tax credit system, . . . America's health care system would be vastly improved, and most of its current problems would eventually solve themselves.**

Nina Owcharenko, who is a senior policy analyst with the Heritage Foundation, also strongly believes in a consumer-driven health care system. She is convinced that this could be accomplished by reforming the current tax code and implementing a universal tax credit program. She explains the advantage:

> A fixed tax credit offers a flat dollar amount to be applied to a health care premium. . . . Such an approach creates a defined and predictable amount that would be easier to administer and can, depending on the size of the plan deductible, reduce the number of uninsured by up to 85 percent. It would also make recipients more sensitive to

the price of the policies they purchase, encouraging them to choose a plan based on value.[42]

Owcharenko and others who share her preference for a tax credit–based health care system say that it could easily be financed by revamping the existing tax structure. For instance, employers currently receive a huge tax deduction from the federal government for the money they pay for their employees' health insurance benefits. If this were eliminated, it would free up money that could be used for the tax credits. In addition, employers can legally exclude the value of health care benefits from their workers' wages—and there is no cap on the dollar amount. That means employees are not taxed on their insurance benefits as they are on their wages, no matter how expensive those benefits may be. As a result, says Owcharenko, "the more generous the health benefit, the greater the amount that is exempt from taxation."[43] By taxing these benefits as income, additional revenues would be generated for health care tax credits. Owcharenko adds that workers who do not have employer-based coverage do not receive the same federal tax benefits and must use after-tax dollars to pay for health insurance and medical expenses. This, she believes, is an example of another egregious flaw in America's current health care system.

Numerous people share Owcharenko's beliefs in the advantages of a health care system based on tax credits. In addition to the obvious benefit of the uninsured being able to afford health insurance for themselves and their families, people would no longer feel as though they must stay in a job simply out of fear of losing their insurance benefits.

> **Under [one] plan, all residents of the United States would receive a health care voucher good for the acquisition of health coverage through a qualified plan or insurance company of their choice.**

Because they would own and pay for their own policy, they could take it with them if they change jobs or quit working. Another advantage is that people would not have to settle for whatever health plan their employer chooses. Instead, they could choose the individual plan, doctors, and medical services that they preferred, which would stimulate healthy competition among insurers, medical providers, and hospitals. This would naturally keep costs in check and improve quality as providers competed for customers. With the tax credit system, Owcharenko is convinced that America's health care system would be vastly improved, and most of its current problems would eventually solve themselves. She writes: "Individual health care tax credits, in combination with a robust market for insurance products, would offer individuals the opportunity to secure private health care coverage of their own, moving the system closer to a consumer-oriented model that is fairer and more transparent and that empowers individuals to make health care decisions for themselves and their families."[44]

> " Republican, Democratic, and Independent legislators in the United States have been haggling over the health care issue for decades, but unfortunately they have made little or no progress. "

Health Care Vouchers

As a practicing physician, Ezekiel Emanuel has been very interested in health care reform for many years. He has developed a plan that he believes would be both affordable and effective in repairing the U.S. health care problems and eliminating the disparity that currently exists between the wealthy and the working poor. Under Emanuel's plan, all residents of the United States would receive a health care voucher good for the acquisition of health coverage through a qualified plan or insurance company of their choice. The voucher would not be equivalent to cash; rather, it would be an insurance voucher that entitled the holder to health care benefits. There would be no restrictions on enrollment requirements, nor would there be any exclusions for preexisting conditions. Emanuel's vision is that the health benefits would be generous, modeled after those currently provided to employees of the federal government through the Federal Employees Health Benefits Program.

The new system would be financed, in part, by the elimination of the tax exemption for employer-based health insurance. Additional funding would come from a value-added tax, possibly a sales tax on purchases of goods and services. Although Americans would likely balk at more taxes, Emanuel says that the new tax would be more than offset by the elimination of taxes that are currently paid to support Medicare and Medicaid (both of which would eventually be phased out), as well as monies that are spent on insurance premiums, copayments, and deductibles. Americans, he believes, would be much better off financially under his system—and those who currently lack medical care because they are uninsured would no longer have to suffer or fear for their families' future.

What Is the Solution?

Republican, Democratic, and Independent legislators in the United States have been haggling over the health care issue for decades, but unfortunately, they have made little or no progress. America's health care system has steadily declined over the years in terms of affordability and quality—and the stark reality is that today some 46 million Americans have no insurance, millions of others are underinsured, and many, many more fear that they will lose their health insurance or go bankrupt because they cannot pay medical costs. So what is the answer? Can this problem be solved? Is a solution within reach? Although it will take a great deal of time and effort, legislators and other decision makers will hopefully resolve their differences and arrive at a plan that ensures quality health care for all. If they cannot, the health care situation in the United States may become even bleaker than it already is.

How Can America Improve Its Health Care System?

❝I believe we can reduce costs and improve the quality of care by increasing competition. We can do it through tax cuts, not tax hikes. We can do it by empowering patients and their doctors, not government bureaucrats.❞

—Rudolph Giuliani, "A Free-Market Cure for US Healthcare System," *Boston Globe*, August 3, 2007. www.boston.com.

Giuliani is the former mayor of New York City.

❝When it comes to health care, it's a government bureaucracy [the Veterans Administration] that's setting the standard for maintaining best practices while reducing costs, and it's the private sector that's lagging in quality.❞

—Phillip Longman, "The Best Care Anywhere," *Washington Monthly*, January/February 2005. www.washingtonmonthly.com.

Longman is Schwartz Senior Fellow at the New America Foundation and the author of *The Empty Cradle*.

Bracketed quotes indicate conflicting positions.

* Editor's Note: While the definition of a primary source can be narrowly or broadly defined, for the purposes of Compact Research, a primary source consists of: 1) results of original research presented by an organization or researcher; 2) eyewitness accounts of events, personal experience, or work experience; 3) first-person editorials offering pundits' opinions; 4) government officials presenting political plans and/or policies; 5) representatives of organizations presenting testimony or policy.

Primary Source Quotes

66 Herein lies the fundamental economic principle that explains why health care costs are growing much faster than the rate of inflation: cost insulation. . . . When we as consumers are insulated from the cost of our purchasing decisions, we tend to consume more. 99

—Merrill Matthews, "What Drives the High Cost of Health Care," *U.S. Chamber Magazine*, March 2008. www.uschambermagazine.com.

Matthews is executive director of the Council for Affordable Health Insurance.

66 'Moral hazard' is the term economists use to describe the fact that insurance can change the behavior of the person being insured. . . . The moral hazard argument makes sense, however, only if we consume health care in the same way that we consume other consumer goods, and to economists like [John] Nyman this assumption is plainly absurd. 99

—Malcolm Gladwell, "The Moral-Hazard Myth," *New Yorker*, August 29, 2005. www.newyorker.com.

Gladwell is a staff writer with the *New Yorker* magazine.

66 The U.S. health care system is in the midst of a ferocious war. . . . The American people must win this battle. A system controlled by the insurance companies or hospitals or government will kill us financially and medically. 99

—Regina Herzlinger, *Who Killed Health Care?* New York: McGraw-Hill, 2007, p. 1.

Herzlinger is a health care analyst and author.

66 Electronic health records (EHRs) are promising tools to improve quality and efficiency in health care. 99

—Ashish K. Jha et al., "How Common Are Electronic Health Records in the United States? A Summary of the Evidence," *Health Affairs*, October 11, 2006, p. 496.

Jha is assistant professor of health policy and management at Harvard University.

> **Electronic health record (EHR) advocates argue that EHRs lead to reduced errors and reduced costs. Many reports suggest otherwise.**

—Jaan Sidorov, "It Ain't Necessarily So: The Electronic Health Record and the Unlikely Prospect of Reducing Health Care Costs," *Health Affairs*, July/August 2008, p. 1,079.

Sidorov is an associate in the Department of General Internal Medicine at Geisinger Medical Center in Danville, Pennsylvania, and medical director of care coordination.

> **Exactly when Americans will finally abandon their Alice-in-Wonderland, ostrich-like refusal to face the realities of their health care mess is anyone's guess.**

—Andrew Stephen, "Sick: The Great American Con Trick," *New Statesman*, October 8, 2007, pp. 34–35.

Stephen is the U.S. editor of *New Statesman* and a contributor to BBC news programs and the *Sunday Times Magazine*.

> **Consumer-driven health care has powerful enemies, the status quo fat cats or single-payer ideologues who spin powerful, seductive tales about its dangers.**

—Regina Herzlinger, *Who Killed Health Care?* New York: McGraw-Hill, 2007, p. 256.

Herzlinger is a Harvard University business professor and health care analyst.

> **Healthcare providers and patients must speak up and demand that our elected officials make health insurance industry reform a priority.**

—Orville Campbell, "Health Insurance Companies—Their Abuse and Tricks," eZine Articles, January 11, 2008. http://ezinearticles.com.

Campbell is an internist from Atlanta, Georgia.

66 This profusion of proposals means that health care is getting more attention, and this makes reform more likely. But these proposals are like band-aids and fall far short of what our sick health-care system needs. **99**

—Ezekiel J. Emanuel and Victor R. Fuchs, "Beyond Health-Care Band-Aids," *Washington Post*, February 7, 2008. www.washingtonpost.com.

Emanuel is chairman of the Department of Clinical Bioethics at the National Institutes of Health Clinical Center; Fuchs is a former president of the American Economics Association.

66 Nurses believe that health care is a right, not a privilege. **99**

—Karen Ballard, "Increasing Access to Health Insurance Coverage and Moving Toward Universal Healthcare Coverage," testimony before the New York State Departments of Health and Insurance, October 30, 2007. www.nysna.org.

Ballard is a registered nurse and president of the New York State Nurses Association.

66 Trying to create a universal 'right' to health care turns patients into pieces of meat and turns doctors into slaves. **99**

—Paul Hsieh, "Two Arguments Why Health Care Is Not a Right," letter to the editor, *Denver Post*, April 30, 2007. www.denverpost.com.

Hsieh is a physician from Sedalia, Colorado.

Facts and Illustrations

How Can America Improve Its Health Care System?

- The Commonwealth Fund anticipates that the number of uninsured Americans will rise to **56 million** by 2013.

- According to a survey by the AFL/CIO, **94 percent** of insured respondents said that America's health care system needs fundamental change or to be rebuilt.

- At the current growth rate, U.S. health care spending is projected to reach **$3 trillion** by 2011 and **$4.2 trillion** by 2016.

- The Centers for Medicare and Medicaid Services projects that health spending will be nearly one-fifth of GDP, or **19.6 percent**, by 2016.

- Medicare spending is expected to reach **$500 billion** by 2012 and **$884 billion** by 2017, up from $427 billion in 2007.

- According to Medicare program trustees, under the current payment structure, Medicare's Hospital Insurance Trust Fund will be **insolvent by 2019**.

- The *Journal of Health Care Finance* states that **medical tourism** is on the rise; in 2005 alone, more than **55,000 Americans** visited the Bumrungrad Hospital in Thailand for elective surgery procedures.

Health Care Concerns for the Future

As the health care system has continued to deteriorate, with soaring costs and the number of uninsured or underinsured increasing each year, people in the United States want legislators to make health care a top priority. These charts show how Americans responded to questions asked in a February 2007 joint poll by the *New York Times* and CBS News.

Which of these domestic policies is most important for the President and Congress to concentrate on right now?

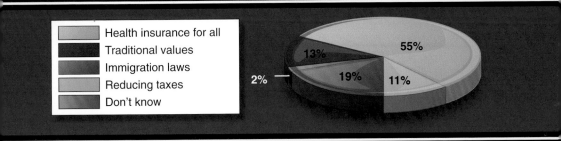

Legend:
- Health insurance for all
- Traditional values
- Immigration laws
- Reducing taxes
- Don't know

55% / 13% / 11% / 19% / 2%

How serious a problem is it for the United States that many Americans do not have health insurance?

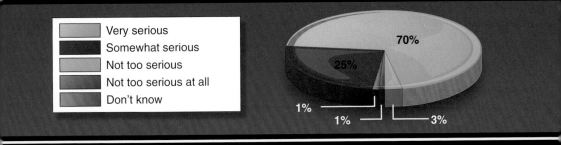

Legend:
- Very serious
- Somewhat serious
- Not too serious
- Not too serious at all
- Don't know

70% / 25% / 1% / 1% / 3%

Would you be willing or not willing to pay higher taxes so that all Americans have health insurance that they can't lose no matter what?

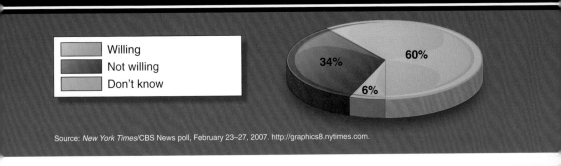

Legend:
- Willing
- Not willing
- Don't know

60% / 34% / 6%

Source: *New York Times*/CBS News poll, February 23–27, 2007. http://graphics8.nytimes.com.

Health Care Cost Growth

Many economists warn that if America's health care system is not radically reformed, and costs are not brought under control, the system will inevitably collapse. This graph illustrates actual and projected cost increases by source, including public and private sources, and individual out-of-pocket payments.

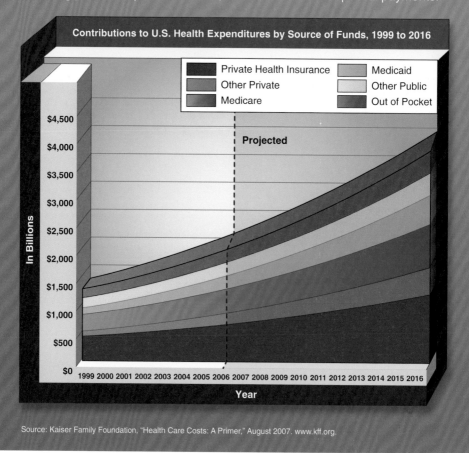

Source: Kaiser Family Foundation, "Health Care Costs: A Primer," August 2007. www.kff.org.

- Health economist Andrea Sisko states that hospital spending will rise from **$697 billion** in 2007 to more than $1.3 trillion in 2017, and drug spending will increase from $231 billion to nearly **$516 billion**.

- The Centers for Medicare and Medicaid Services projects that Medicaid will continue to grow at an average of **7.9 percent** per year, from $361.2 billion in 2008 to $717.3 billion by 2017.

Employer-Provided Health Insurance Costs Soaring

One of the biggest problems with America's health care system is that costs are out of control, including the cost of health insurance. Growing numbers of businesses in the United States are either reducing insurance benefits, passing more of the cost along to employees, or eliminating the benefits altogether—and if premiums continue to rise as they have consistently done over the years, more employers will be forced to do the same. This graph shows how costs have spiked since 1999.

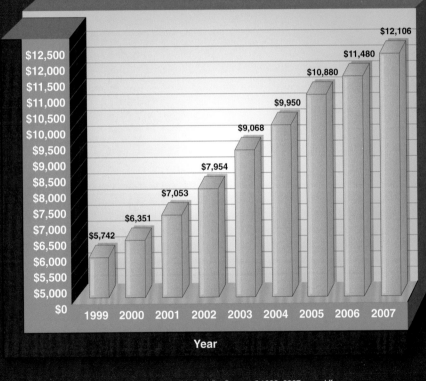

Average Annual Premiums for Employer-Provided Family Health Insurance 1999–2007

Year	Premium
1999	$5,742
2000	$6,351
2001	$7,053
2002	$7,954
2003	$9,068
2004	$9,950
2005	$10,880
2006	$11,480
2007	$12,106

Source: Kaiser Family Foundation, "Employer Health Benefits Surveys," 1999–2007. www.kff.org.

- A 2008 *Health Sciences* report by Deloitte states that U.S. health care costs are growing at **8 percent** per year, which will force employers to find ways to control health care expenses or stop providing health benefits to employees altogether.

Americans Dissatisfied with U.S. Health Care System

Although U.S. legislators often talk publicly about the importance of health care reform, they do not agree on the best way to fix the current system, and the problems continue to grow worse. According to a November 2007 Gallup poll, people in the United States are not happy about America's health care system.

Are you generally satisfied with the total cost of health care in this country?

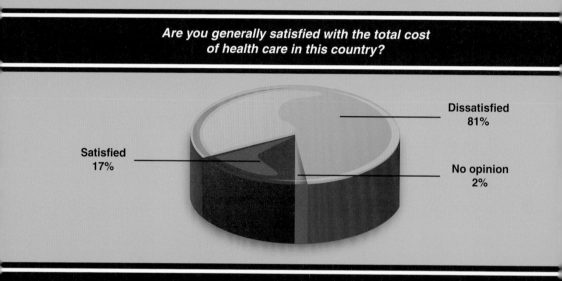

Dissatisfied
81%

Satisfied
17%

No opinion
2%

Which of these statements do you think best describes the U.S. health care system today—it is in a state of crisis, it has major problems, it has minor problems, or it does not have any problems?

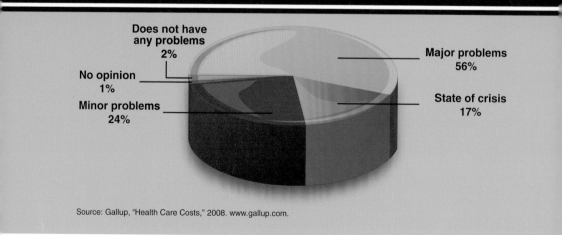

Does not have any problems
2%

No opinion
1%

Minor problems
24%

Major problems
56%

State of crisis
17%

Source: Gallup, "Health Care Costs," 2008. www.gallup.com.

- Deloitte projects that existing **shortages in nursing** and primary care will continue to adversely affect health care access and quality.

- Consulting firm Booz Allen Hamilton predicts that **significant change** in America's health care system is unlikely prior to 2010 and is likely to be gradual thereafter.

Key People and Advocacy Groups

Americans for Free Choice in Medicine (AFCM): An educational organization, the AFCM advocates individual rights, personal responsibility, and free market economics in the health care industry.

Centers for Medicare and Medicaid Services (CMS): Part of the U.S. Department of Health and Human Services, CMS seeks to ensure effective, up-to-date health care coverage and to promote quality care for Medicare and Medicaid beneficiaries.

Hillary Rodham Clinton: In 1993 Clinton, who was then First Lady of the United States, led a task force that developed a health care reform package; the plan was later defeated by Congress.

The Commonwealth Fund: A private foundation, the fund supports independent research on health care issues and makes grants to improve health care practices and policies.

Health Care for America Now: A national grassroots campaign, Health Care for America Now is committed to achieving a guarantee of quality, affordable health care for all.

Lyndon Baines Johnson: Sworn in as the thirty-sixth president of the United States after the assassination of John F. Kennedy, Johnson was instrumental in getting the Medicare and Medicaid programs passed in 1965.

National Coalition on Health Care (NCHC): NCHC is an organization that seeks to improve America's health care system through principles of coverage for everyone, cost management, improvement of health care quality and safety, equitable financing, and simplified administration.

Physicians for a National Health Program (PNHP): A group composed of physicians, the PNHP advocates a universal, comprehensive single-payer national health program that serves all people in America.

Harry S. Truman: The thirty-third president of the United States, in 1945 Truman was unsuccessful in requesting that Congress establish a national health insurance plan.

Veterans Health Administration (VHA): A branch of the U.S. Department of Veterans Affairs, the VHA administers benefits, including health care, to current and retired military personnel.

World Health Organization (WHO): Among WHO's goals are to provide leadership on global health matters, shape the health research agenda, and monitor and assess world health trends.

Chronology

1900
The average life expectancy in the United States is 47 years.

1921
The Veterans Bureau is established to consolidate veterans' affairs; its name is later changed to the Veterans Administration (VA).

1942
To prevent employers from using wages to compete for a labor force in short supply because of World War II, Congress passes the Stabilization Act, which limits wage increases but permits the adoption of employee insurance plans.

1959
The U.S. Congress passes the Federal Employees Health Benefits Act to provide taxpayer-funded health insurance to federal employees and their families.

1900 1920 1940 1960

1929
A group of teachers from Dallas contract with Baylor Hospital to provide 21 days of hospitalization for a fixed payment of $6; this is the precursor to Blue Cross Blue Shield.

1932
The National Labor Relations Act, requiring management to bargain with labor over "wages and conditions," is enacted; it will eventually become a catalyst for employer-provided health benefits.

1940
Fewer than 10 percent of Americans have health insurance coverage; the majority pay their medical expenses out of pocket.

1950
National health care expenditures are 4.5 percent of America's gross domestic product (GDP).

1945
The United Nations Conference in San Francisco unanimously approves the establishment of a new, autonomous international health organization that is later named the World Health Organization (WHO).

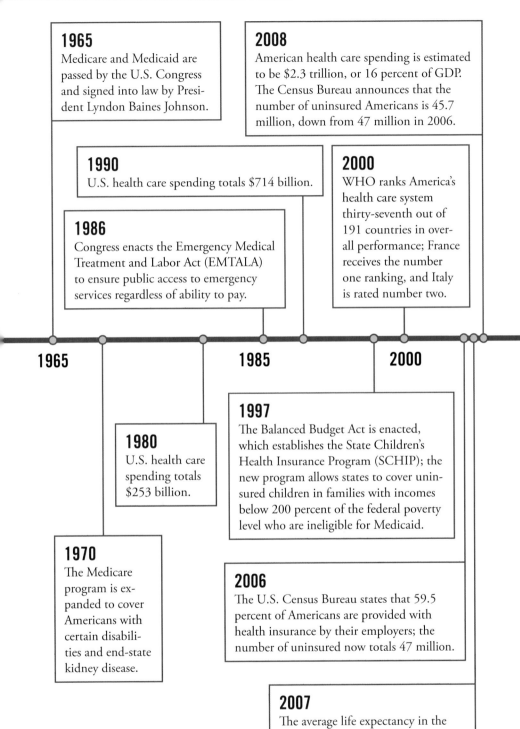

1965
Medicare and Medicaid are passed by the U.S. Congress and signed into law by President Lyndon Baines Johnson.

2008
American health care spending is estimated to be $2.3 trillion, or 16 percent of GDP. The Census Bureau announces that the number of uninsured Americans is 45.7 million, down from 47 million in 2006.

1990
U.S. health care spending totals $714 billion.

2000
WHO ranks America's health care system thirty-seventh out of 191 countries in overall performance; France receives the number one ranking, and Italy is rated number two.

1986
Congress enacts the Emergency Medical Treatment and Labor Act (EMTALA) to ensure public access to emergency services regardless of ability to pay.

1965　　1985　　2000

1997
The Balanced Budget Act is enacted, which establishes the State Children's Health Insurance Program (SCHIP); the new program allows states to cover uninsured children in families with incomes below 200 percent of the federal poverty level who are ineligible for Medicaid.

1980
U.S. health care spending totals $253 billion.

1970
The Medicare program is expanded to cover Americans with certain disabilities and end-state kidney disease.

2006
The U.S. Census Bureau states that 59.5 percent of Americans are provided with health insurance by their employers; the number of uninsured now totals 47 million.

2007
The average life expectancy in the United States has risen to 77.9 years.

Related Organizations

American Medical Association (AMA)

515 N. State St.

Chicago, IL 60610

phone: (312) 464-5199; toll-free (800) 621-8335

fax: (312) 464-5900

e-mail: info@ama-assn.org • Web site: www.ama-assn.org

The AMA's mission is to promote the art and science of medicine and the betterment of public health. A wide variety of materials are offered through its Web site, including speech transcripts, news releases, articles about health care–related issues, and the *American Medical News* newsletter.

Americans for Free Choice in Medicine (AFCM)

1525 Superior Ave., Suite 100

Newport Beach, CA 92663

phone: (949) 645-2622 • fax: (949) 645-4624

e-mail: mail@afcm.org • Web site: www.afcm.org

AFCM is an educational organization that advocates individual rights, personal responsibility, and free-market economics in the health care industry. Its Web site offers numerous articles, news releases, and an opinion-editorial section with archives that date back to 1994.

Brookings Institution

1775 Massachusetts Ave. NW

Washington, DC 20036

phone: (202) 797-6000 • fax: (202) 797-6213

e-mail: communications@brookings.edu

Web site: www.brookings.edu

The Brookings Institution conducts high-quality, independent research that advances its goals of strengthening American democracy, fostering the economic and social welfare of all Americans, and securing a safe, prosperous, and cooperative international system. Available on its Web site are a number of health care–related articles, expert commentaries, and research publications.

Cato Institute

1000 Massachusetts Ave. NW

Washington, DC 20001-5403

phone: (202) 842-0200 • fax: (202) 842-3490

Web site: www.cato.org

Cato is a libertarian organization that advocates traditional American principles of limited government, individual liberty, free markets, and peace. Its Web site offers an extensive array of health care–related materials, including commentaries, policy studies, journals, and a newsletter titled *Cato's Letter*, as well as a daily podcast and a weekly video.

Centers for Medicare and Medicaid Services (CMS)

7500 Security Blvd.

Baltimore, MD 21244

phone: (410) 786-3000; toll free: (877) 267-2323

Web site: www.cms.hhs.gov

CMS seeks to ensure effective, up-to-date health care coverage and to promote quality care for Medicare and Medicaid beneficiaries. Its vision is a transformed and modern health care system in the United States. The organization's Web site offers statistics, trends, and reports, and its search engine leads to numerous health care publications.

The Commonwealth Fund

1 E. Seventy-fifth St.

New York, NY 10021

phone: (212) 606-3800 • fax: (212) 606-3500

e-mail: info@cmwf.org • Web site: www.commonwealthfund.org

The Commonwealth Fund is a private foundation that supports independent research on health care issues and makes grants to improve health care practices and policies. Its Web site features numerous health care publications such as surveys, charts, state scorecards, newsletters, and a special "Topics" section that addresses various health care issues.

Health Care for America Now

1825 K St. NW, Suite 400

Washington, DC 20006

phone: (202) 955-5665

e-mail : info@healthcareforamericanow.org

Web site: healthcareforamericanow.org

Health Care for America Now is a national grassroots campaign committed to achieving a guarantee of quality, affordable health care for all. Its Web site features news articles, media advisories, and a link to the Now! blog.

National Coalition on Health Care (NCHC)

1120 G St. NW, Suite 810

Washington, DC 20005

phone: (202) 638-7151

e-mail: info@nchc.org • Web site: www.nchc.org

The NCHC seeks to improve America's health care system through principles of coverage for everyone, cost management, improvement of health care quality and safety, equitable financing, and simplified administration. Its Web site offers facts about health care, press releases, information on health care quality and insurance costs, world health care data, studies and reports, and speeches.

National Committee for Quality Assurance (NCQA)

1100 13th St. NW, Suite 1000

Washington, DC 20005

phone: (202) 955-3500 • fax: (202) 955-3599

Web site: www.ncqa.org

The NCQA is a nonprofit organization that is dedicated to improving health care quality. Its Web site offers health care report cards, policy updates, research and reports, and news articles.

Physicians for a National Health Program (PNHP)

29 E. Madison St., Suite 602

Chicago, IL 60602

phone: (312) 782-6006 • fax: (312) 782-6007

e-mail: info@pnhp.org • Web site: www.pnhp.org

PNHP, which has more than 15,000 members and chapters through-out the United States, advocates a universal, comprehensive single-payer national health program that serves people in America. Its Web site includes timely news articles, press releases, a PNHP student forum section, frequently asked questions about health care, and a link to "PNHP on Facebook."

World Health Organization (WHO)

Avenue Appia 20

1211 Geneva 27

Switzerland

phone: +41 22 791 21 11 • fax: +41 22 791 31 11

Web site: www.who.int

WHO describes itself as "the directing and coordinating authority for health within the United Nations system." The organization seeks to provide leadership on global health matters, shape the health research agenda, set norms and standards for health care, articulate evidence-based policy options, provide technical support to countries, and monitor and assess health trends. Its Web site offers the *World Health Report*, as well as health care data and statistics, information on numerous health-related topics, and country-specific information on health care.

For Further Research

Books

Donald L. Bartlett and James B. Steele, *Critical Condition: How Health Care in America Became Big Business—and Bad Medicine*. New York: Doubleday, 2004.

Shannon Brownlee, *Overtreated: Why Too Much Medicine Is Making Us Sicker and Poorer*. New York: Bloomsbury, 2007.

Jonathan Cohn, *Sick: The Untold Story of America's Health Care Crisis—and the People Who Pay the Price*. New York: HarperCollins, 2007.

David M. Cutler, *Your Money or Your Life: Strong Medicine for America's Health Care System*. New York: Oxford University Press, 2004.

Ezekiel J. Emanuel, *Healthcare, Guaranteed*. New York: PublicAffairs, 2008.

David Gratzer, *The Cure: How Capitalism Can Save American Health Care*. New York: Encounter, 2006.

Regina Herzlinger, *Who Killed Health Care?* New York: McGraw-Hill, 2007.

Arnold Kling, *Crisis of Abundance: Rethinking How We Pay for Health Care*. Washington, DC: Cato Institute, 2006.

Kant Patel and Mark E. Rushefsky, *Health Care Politics and Policy in America*. Armonk, NY: M.E. Sharpe, 2006.

Michael E. Porter and Elizabeth Olmsted Teisberg, *Redefining Health Care*. Boston: Harvard Business School Press, 2006.

Arnold Relman, *A Second Opinion: Rescuing America's Health Care*. New York, PublicAffairs, 2007.

Julius B. Richmond and Rashi Fein, *The Health Care Mess: How We Got into It and What It Will Take to Get Out*. Cambridge, MA: Harvard University Press, 2005.

Periodicals

Steve Abell, "Managing the Cost of Health Care in America: Ensuring Quality, Value and Access, *Arkansas Business*, May 5, 2008.

James Capretta, "Dr. O'Bama's Prescription Isn't One We Should Want to Take," *National Review*, September 1, 2008.

Geoff Colvin, "We All Pay for the Uninsured," *Fortune*, May 12, 2008.

Denis Cortese and Robert Smoldt, "A Health System by Design," *Modern Healthcare*, September 24, 2007.

Duncan Currie, "Changing Doctors: Health Care Reform Is Coming. The Only Question Is What Kind," *Weekly Standard*, October 18, 2007.

Theodore Dalrymple, "Health of the State: Doctors, Patients, and Michael Moore," *National Review*, August 13, 2007.

Mary Jane England, "Diagnosing the U.S. Health Care System," *America*, December 3, 2007.

Dana A. Forgione and Pamela C. Smith, "Medical Tourism and Its Impact on the U.S. Health Care System," *Journal of Health Care Finance*, Fall 2007.

Joyce Frieden, "Health Care Reform 'Possible' Despite Economic Slump," *Family Practice News*, May 15, 2008.

Jason Furman, "Health Reform Through Tax Reform: A Primer," *Health Affairs*, May/June 2008.

Aaron McCarroll Gallegos, "Healing and the Common Good: Six Myths About Single-Payer Health Care," *Sojourners*, August 2008.

Peter Glusker, "Universal Health Care That's Not-for-Profit Can Work," *National Catholic Reporter*, September 21, 2007.

Erik Goldman, "It's Baaaaad Out There: Healthcare Is in the Poorest State It's Ever Been, and It's About to Get Worse," *Nutraceuticals World*, October 1, 2007.

Mary Kay Henry, "A Matter of Life and Death: Health Care for All Is a Moral Imperative," *Sojourners*, August 2008.

Stanton R. Mehr, "Is Our Health-Care System Sick? What Teens Need to Know About Health Insurance," *Current Health 2*, January 2008.

Barack Obama, "My Cure for an Ailing System," *Modern Healthcare*, November 26, 2007.

John O'Sullivan, "Risky Operation: Socialized Medicine Comes at a Cost," *National Review*, August 27, 2007.

Jennifer Pellet, "A Prescription for Health Care: What Can Be Done to Improve the Cost and Quality of Medical Care," *Chief Executive*, December 2007.

Ramesh Ponnuru, "Everything You Always Wanted to Know About Health Care: But Were Afraid to Ask," *National Review*, September 24, 2007.

Robert D. Reischauer, "Benefits with Risks—Bush's Tax-Based Health Care Proposals, *New England Journal of Medicine*, April 5, 2007.

Emad Rizk, "Creating Transparency, One Step at a Time," *Health Management Technology*, September 2007.

Diane Rowland and Adele Shartzer, "Federal Health Coverage Programs: Building Blocks for Coverage of the Uninsured," *National Voter*, February 2008.

Joseph W. Thompson, "Affordable Access to Health Care: Everyone's Problem," *Arkansas Business*, May 5, 2008.

Darrell E. White, "Help for Health Care System Not a Simple Fix," *Crain's Cleveland Business*, August 20, 2007.

Internet Sources

Sharon Begley, "The Myth of 'Best in the World,'" *Newsweek*, March 22, 2008. www.newsweek.com/id/128635.

Victoria Colliver, "In Critical Condition: Health Care in America," *San Francisco Chronicle*, October 11, 2004. www.sfgate.com/cgi-bin/article.cgi?file=/c/a/2004/10/11/MNGII96CVP1.DTL.

Wendy Diller, "Implications of Health Care Reform," *BusinessWeek*, July 25, 2008. www.businessweek.com/investor/content/jul2008/pi20080725_983150.htm?chan=rss_topDiscussed_ssi_5.

Chris Farrell, "Health Care: The Real Fiscal Nightmare," *Business-Week*, August 20, 2008. www.businessweek.com/investor/content/aug2008/pi20080818_318145.htm?campaign_id=rss_daily.

David R. Francis, "Health Care Crisis Countdown," *Christian Science Monitor*, November 6, 2006. www.csmonitor.com/2006/1106/p16s01-cogn.html.

Frontline, "Sick Around the World," PBS, October 25, 2007. www.pbs.org/wgbh/pages/frontline/sickaroundtheworld.

Lisa Girion, "Health Insurer Tied Bonuses to Dropping Sick Policyholders," *Los Angeles Times*, November 9, 2007. www.latimes.com/business/la-fi-insure9nov09,0,4409342.story.

Malcolm Gladwell, "The Moral-Hazard Myth," *New Yorker*, August 29, 2005. www.newyorker.com/archive/2005/08/29/050829fa_fact.

Suzanne Goldenberg, "Expensive and Divisive: How America Is Losing Patience with a Failing System," *Guardian*, September 13, 2007. www.guardian.co.uk/world/2007/sep/13/usa.health.

Andrew Gumbel, "Surviving the U.S. Health Care System," *Seattle Post-Intelligencer*, June 29, 2007. seattlepi.nwsource.com/opinion/321839_focussicko01.html.

Kaiser Family Foundation, "Health Care Costs: A Primer," August 2007. www.kff.org/insurance/upload/7670.pdf.

John McCain, "The Right Rx," *National Review*, May 1, 2008. http://article.nationalreview.com/?q=OWE0ZWJiMGY1OWFiNDk2NDRhNGQwMTM3MjExZjM3NWE=.

Jane Bryant Quinn, "Yes, We Can All Be Insured," *Newsweek*, August 15, 2007. www.newsweek.com/id/32858.

John Stossel and Andrew Sullivan, "American Health Care in Critical Condition," ABC News, September 11, 2007. abcnews.go.com/2020/Stossel/story?id=3580676.

Thomas Szasz, "The Myth of Health Insurance, *Freeman*, May 2003. www.fee.org/pdf/the-freeman/szasz0503.pdf.

World Health Organization, "World Health Report: A Safer Future," 2007. www.who.int/whr/2007/whr07_en.pdf.

Source Notes

Overview

1. Quoted in John Bonifield, "Dying for Lack of Insurance," CNN, April 25, 2008. www.cnn.com.
2. Jane Bryant Quinn, "Health Care's New Lottery," *Newsweek*, February 27, 2006. www.newsweek.com.
3. Quoted in *Crain's Cleveland Business*, "Help for Health Care System Not a Simple Fix," August 20, 2007, p. 10.
4. Quoted in Public Citizen, "Study Shows National Health Insurance Could Save $286 Billion on Health Care Paperwork," January 14, 2004. www.citizen.org.
5. Joel A. Harrison, "Paying More, Getting Less," *Dollars and Sense*, May/June 2008. www.dollarsandsense.org.
6. Harrison, "Paying More, Getting Less."
7. Jane Bryant Quinn, "Yes, We Can All Be Insured," *Newsweek*, August 15, 2007. www.newsweek.com.
8. Quoted in Patrick Sawer, "Health-Care Failings Make Britain the Poor Relation Within Europe," *Sunday Telegraph*, November 11, 2007. www.telegraph.co.uk.
9. Ezekiel J. Emanuel, *Healthcare, Guaranteed*. New York: PublicAffairs, 2008, p. 1.
10. Quinn, "Yes, We Can All Be Insured."

What Is the State of America's Health Care System?

11. Michael E. Porter and Elizabeth Olmsted Teisberg, *Redefining Health Care*. Boston: Harvard Business School Press, 2006, pp. 1–2.
12. David M. Schwartz, "How Much Is a Trillion?" National Public Radio, February 8, 2008. www.npr.org.
13. Quoted in Victoria Colliver, "In Critical Condition: Health Care in America, *San Francisco Chronicle*, October 11, 2004. www.sfgate.com.
14. David Asman, "There's No Place Like Home," *Wall Street Journal*, June 8, 2005. www.opinionjournal.com.
15. Orville Campbell, "Health Insurance Companies—Their Abuse and Tricks," World Health Blog, January 11, 2008. http://toyourhealth.healthandwellnessmarketing.com.
16. Quoted in California Nurses Association, "RN's Statement on Death of Nataline Sarkisyan: 'CIGNA Should Have Listened to her Doctors and Approved the Transplant a Week Ago,'" Bio-Medicine, December 21, 2007. www.bio-medicine.org.
17. John Stossel and Andrew Sullivan, "American Health Care in Critical Condition," ABC News, September 11, 2007. http://abcnews.go.com.
18. Shannon Brownlee, "Why Does Health Care Cost So Much?" *AARP Magazine*, July/August 2008. www.aarpmagazine.org.

Who Suffers Most Under America's Health Care System?

19. Quoted in Sarah Boseley, "Expensive and Divisive: How America Is Losing Patience with a Failing System," *Guardian*, September 13, 2007. www.guardian.co.uk.
20. Sara R. Collins et al., "Losing Ground: How the Loss of Adequate Health Insurance Is Burdening Working Families," Commonwealth Fund, August 2008. www.commonwealthfund.org.
21. Malcolm Gladwell, "The Moral-Hazard Myth," *New Yorker*, August 29, 2005. www.newyorker.com.

22. Quoted in Johns Hopkins Bloomberg School of Public Health, "Hospitals Charge Uninsured and 'Self-Pay' Patients More than Double What Insured Patients Pay," news release, May 8, 2007. www.jhsph.edu.
23. Quoted in Chad Terhune, "Medical Bills You Shouldn't Pay," *BusinessWeek*, August 28, 2008. www.businessweek.com.
24. Quoted in Terhune, "Medical Bills You Shouldn't Pay."
25. Annette B. Ramírez de Arellano and Sidney M. Wolfe, "Unsettling Scores: A Ranking of State Medicaid Programs," Public Citizen Health Research Group, April 2007. www2.citizen.org.
26. Ramírez de Arellano and Wolfe, "Unsettling Scores."
27. Patricia H. White and Brenda Dane, "No Net: Pharmacy Board's 'Safety' Rule Would Harm Low-Income Patients," *Charleston Gazette*, August 24, 2008. http://wvgazette.com.

Should America's Health Care Be Nationalized?

28. George W. Bush, "The Third Bush-Kerry Presidential Debate," Commission on Presidential Debates, October 13, 2004. www.debates.org.
29. Quoted in Julie Appleby, "U.S. Health Insurers Suggest Swiss, Dutch as Prototypes," *USA Today*, October 31, 2007. www.usatoday.com.
30. Stossel and Sullivan, "American Health Care in Critical Condition."
31. Asman, "There's No Place Like Home."
32. Richard Knox, "Most Patients Happy with German Health Care," National Public Radio, July 3, 2008. www.npr.org.
33. Knox, "Most Patients Happy with German Health Care."
34. Karl Lauterbach, "Sick Around the World," *Frontline*, Public Broadcasting Service, October 25, 2007. www.pbs.org.
35. Harris Interactive, "Health Care Systems in Ten Developed Countries: The U.S. System Is Most Unpopular and Dutch System the Most Popular," July 2, 2008. www.harrisinteractive.com.
36. Robert J. Kuttner, "Market-Based Failure—a Second Opinion on U.S. Health Care Costs," *New England Journal of Medicine*, February 7, 2008, p. 551.

How Can America Improve Its Health Care System?

37. Porter and Teisberg, *Redefining Health Care*, p. 381.
38. Porter and Teisberg, *Redefining Health Care*, p. 381.
39. George W. Bush, "President Bush Delivers State of the Union Address," White House, January 23, 2007. www.whitehouse.gov.
40. Quoted in Christopher Lee and Lori Montgomery, "Experts Examine Bush Health Plan," *Washington Post*, January 25, 2007. www.washingtonpost.com.
41. Regina Herzlinger, *Who Killed Health Care?* New York: McGraw-Hill, 2007, p. 3.
42. Nina Owcharenko, "Health Care Tax Credits: Designing an Alternative to Employer-Based Coverage," Heritage Foundation, November 8, 2005. www.heritage.org.
43. Owcharenko, "Health Care Tax Credits."
44. Owcharenko, "Health Care Tax Credits."

List of Illustrations

List of Illustrations

Index

About the Author

Peggy J. Parks holds a bachelor of science degree from Aquinas College in Grand Rapids, Michigan, where she graduated magna cum laude. She is an author who has written more than 70 nonfiction educational books for children and young adults, as well as self-published her own cookbook called *Welcome Home: Recipes, Memories, and Traditions from the Heart.* Parks lives in Muskegon, Michigan, a town that she says inspires her writing because of its location on the shores of Lake Michigan.